From Religion to Revival

Establish a Lifestyle of Confidence and Intimacy with Christ

Majisty E. Dennis

From Religion to Revival: Establish a Lifestyle of Confidence and Intimacy with Christ

Copyright© 2017 Majisty E. Dennis

Published by Brown & Duncan Brand, LLC.

Printed in the United States of America.

Library of Congress Cataloging-in-Publication Data

Dennis, Majisty, E.

From Religion To Revival: Establish a Lifestyle of Confidence and Intimacy with Christ / Majisty Dennis

ISBN: 978-0-9984756-7-7

For permissions requests or bulk orders contact Majisty Ministries at MajistyMinistries@gmail.com

All scripture quotations, unless otherwise noted are from the New King James Version® . Copyright©1902 by Thomas Nelson. Used by permission. All rights reserved.

Dedication

This book is dedicated to all who have been mishandled in the process of seeking God's will. I pray this book will serve as an opportunity to heal and move forward.

I also dedicate this book to everyone who does not recognize their greatness. This is your opportunity to open your eyes and see God's great intention when He created you.

If you lack confidence, now is your time to realize that God is for you. Now is the time for you to reap the rewards of confidence in God.

TABLE OF CONTENTS

Acknowledgments

Foreword

Preface

Confidence Concordance

About the Author

Acknowledgements

To God, my Father, You have been there every step of the way. Thank you for revealing yourself to me.

I would like to acknowledge my family for all of the love and support you have given me through the years. I cherish your countless investments in me whether through words of wisdom, time, or love. I love you more than you know!

I would like to acknowledge my book coach Natasha T. Brown. Thank you for being with me in this process and making this book come to life.

Foreword

by

Jekalyn Carr

Grammy Nominated Gospel Recording Artist and Preacher

I thank God for giving Majisty this powerful message to release to the body of Christ. *From Religion to Revival* teaches us the importance of knowing God for ourselves and not just knowing Him based off of the things we've heard.

While reading this book, you will also get a better understanding that when Christ remains our foundation, we are guaranteed a prosperous and successful life, both spiritually and naturally. You will also gain knowledge of knowing God outside of the four walls of the church. This is very important to know, because our lifestyles are what should speak Jesus, not the [church] buildings.

Finally, you will be inspired and compelled to reach out and share this message with others as you continue your daily walk with Christ Jesus.

Preface

It was my first week of bible college. With my body facing the audience and my head down, I sat at the altar soaking in the Spirit during a worship service. A man approached me. I could not see his face or anything else about him, except that he wore cowboy boots. He came closer and closer. He laid hands on me and said, "Get alone with God when nobody's watching, and don't you dare tell anybody about your alone time with God." Me? Prior to that, I had always found myself in constricted atmospheres. Anytime I thought that I was hearing from God it had to be "confirmed" by leadership, and I was conditioned to believe that what God spoke to me had to benefit the person I was following. That word, from this stranger, meant a lot to me. I knew that I needed to gain confidence in the things that God would speak to me.

For starters, I could not keep telling people everything that I heard God saying. I had a history of doubting God's voice for the convenience of others. The relevance of my relationship with God had always been at the disposal of people's opinions. I realized how much God cared for me when that man laid hands on me. God loved me so much that He sent His word to me through someone who had not damaged or abused me. I thought *to* myself, *God had to send someone random to tell me that, because I am always seeking others' approval and I never really trust God's voice unless I have someone else to confirm my revelations with their own "ditto."* During this crucial season in my life, as I was breaking free from the control of religious leaders, everything had to be private. For years, I would clearly hear the voice of the Lord, but my ideas and His words to me were rejected by people who controlled me.

When I arrived on the campus of Christ for the Nations Institute, at age 20, I was spiritually empty, broken, and in desperate need of God's restoration power. That man in the cowboy boots, who laid hands on me, started the rehabilitation of my identity. That word signified the loosening of religious shackles that had my mind and spirit in bondage. Indeed, the Lord was breaking me out of the vicious cycle of religion.

See, I began prophesying at a very young age. My mother was a pastor of a small, but faithful congregation in our hometown of Tacoma, Washington. My entire family ate, slept, and breathed church. I would always tell my mother and other relatives what the Lord was saying. As a young girl, a close female family member went through a stage of promiscuity, and I would see the men come in and out of our lives, and I would say to her, "Don't take a nap with him."

I preached my first sermon at ten-years-old. Although I had a clear gift and calling at a young age, my close connection with the church and church people planted a lot of doubt within me. People would give me a hard time and speak against my ability to proclaim the Gospel with remarks such as, "You don't have no testimony, you aren't old enough to know anything." I was always confused by this behavior and it was the beginning of what some would call "church hurt." I was conflicted, because I was young and living for God like I had been taught in Sunday School; yet, I was criticized for doing exactly what God calls us to do—live holy. People older than me would imply that I did not know God because I hadn't sinned enough. I never understood how these church leaders could preach holiness, but when I lived holy, I was criticized and told that holiness wasn't enough. Wasn't the gospel supposed to keep me *away* from sin? This was the message that I took from my younger years in church and the reaction I received for living the Word. I never agreed with the, "You haven't made enough bad decisions to know God," types of messages. The kind of pressure these religious leaders put on me made me consider if I needed to go and cause problems for myself or "go out and get a *real* testimony." I never felt like this was fair, and I often wrestled with a feeling that I had not experienced enough of the world to have the authority to speak for God. This was despite the undeniable fact that I had always heard from God very clearly, just out of having a relationship with Him.

One of the most important reasons for me writing this book is to let you know that *your* relationship with God is enough. Whatever your testimony is, whatever your testimony isn't—it is enough. My prophetic anointing and Godly lifestyle came under attack by the religious spirit. My heart's desire is to help others navigate their journey from religion to rehabilitation to revival and move from control to confidence. The spirit of religion usually operates through a person who acts like another mediator between a person and God. Spirits of religion also hide in sets of rules that have nothing to do with knowing God. I know that the spirit of religion is the reason why many church girls stray. So many of them, just like me, were taught to live and do right, but then we are shut down by the very people who've preached "The Good News" to us. It's confusing and hypocritical, and it leaves us wondering, *"Where do I go from here? Regardless of what I do, holiness isn't enough and then if I sin, I'm condemned for messing up the holiness that religion said wasn't good enough for me to know God in the first place. I might as well live life my way. Besides these church people do, and they're still confident enough in their relationships with God."*

It is time to give God more than just church on Sundays. He is calling us to go deeper. Christ's bride must be purified, and the church must be rid of the religious spirit keeping us away from intimacy with the bridegroom.

Chapter 1

Defining Confidence

Chapter One: Defining Confidence

Confidence [Definition]: full trust, belief in the powers, trustworthiness, or reliability of a person or thing. Belief in oneself and one's powers or abilities; self-confidence; assurance. Certitude; assurance

Through a series of strategic, relentless attacks, the enemy snatches our confidence, along with our faith and self-worth. Confidence is a real tangible force. In fact, confidence is a physical presence of what faith looks like manifested in the earth realm. When we are operating in faith, we have more confidence, but unfortunately, many believers fall because confidence is simply a word, or aspiration even, but not a lifestyle and personal trait that many can claim to possess. This lack of confidence within the body of Christ is by design. Many Christians have become timid and weak because of satanic forces that are operating within the church. These forces, which are often rooted in religion and legalism, have snatched the life from many young believers, and it is time to put this work to an end.

One of the lies the enemy wants us to believe is that the works of the spiritual realm cannot be felt or experienced in the physical realm. Spiritual things can very well be physical. In fact, the acts and works that are taking place in the spirit have a direct effect on what's going on in the natural or physical realm. This is why we pray, "Thine kingdom come, thy will be done on earth as it is in heaven." Confidence is important, because it is a reflection of how we exercise our kingdom authority. As believers, we are God's authority in the earth realm. God created us to be like Him and expects us to rule, reign, and have dominion. We have a dominion mandate. When we lack confidence, we step down from the authority God gave to us as individual believers and the body as a whole. To walk in a lack of confidence would be our decision to shy away, deliberately, from the authority that God has given to us. The book of 1 Peter 2:9 tells us, "But you are a chosen generation, a royal priesthood, a holy nation, His own special people, that you may proclaim the praises of Him who called you out of darkness into His marvelous light." Did you hear that? We are supposed to carry ourselves as royalty because we are! Our faith in Christ gives us assurance and reinforcement from the Kingdom of God in all that we do. We can be sure that as long as we love the Lord, everything we set out to do will work out for our good. Romans 8:28 confirms this, "And we know that in all things God works for the good of those who love him, who have been called according to His purpose." So, we do not have to be insecure or timid in our efforts to blaze new trails, pursue our destiny, or walk in God's will for our lives. We have every right to be confident, because of what Christ did for us on the cross. The book of 1 John 5:4-5 states, "For everyone who has been born of God overcomes the world. And this is the victory that has overcome the world-our faith. Who is it that overcomes the world, except the one who believes that Jesus is the Son of God?"

Christ

- Justified us (Romans 3:24)
- Adopted us as sons and daughters (Ephesians 1:5)
- Forgave our sins and forgets our sins (Jeremiah 31:34)
- Made provision for our healing (Isaiah 53:5)
- Gave us power to accumulate wealth (Deuteronomy 8:18)
- Expressed His undying love for us (John 3:16)
- Gave us power (2 Timothy 1:7)

- Made us new (2 Corinthians 5:17)

These works that were accomplished on the cross are not only past tense, but they are present and future tense as well. If we remain on earth, we have dominion over the earth, over our sins, and over the enemy—including the crippling spirit of religion. Let us not forget that we have power through Christ. Power! We are strong in Him, and we are not left to become mere victims of our circumstances. When Christ justified us, it was because Jesus Christ became our righteousness. It is a common tendency for believers to sheepishly approach the throne room of God. So many people come to God in timidity and fear, when this is not *at all* what God calls us to do. The Word of God tells us in Hebrews 4:16, "Let us then approach God's throne of our gracious God. There we will receive his mercy, and we will find grace to help us when we need it most." (NLT). People are hesitant to approach the throne of God because of their own "sinner saved by grace mentality" (a wrong mentality, might I add) that they've been brainwashed to believe. I've heard people say it all too many times, "I'm a sinner saved by grace." That statement is impossible. If you were saved by grace, you are no longer a sinner! Instantaneously at the moment you repent, you exit the "sinner" zone and become a "son" or daughter of God. It's time to change the language. You and I are no longer sinners saved by grace. More accurately, we are saints, who occasionally sin. If we truly believe that we are redeemed by the blood of Jesus Christ, then we will approach God boldly, because we are fully convinced that God sees us just as He sees His Son Jesus.

One of the passages that I love to read is Psalm 91:1-2, "He who dwells in the secret place of the Most High Shall abide under the shadow of the Almighty. I will say of the Lord, 'He is my refuge and my fortress; My God, in Him I will trust.'" No one has any problem making God their refuge. We automatically know to run to God in trouble. The challenge is making the One we run to for refuge our dwelling place as well. We must learn to sustain intimacy with God. When we sustain intimacy with God, intimacy will sustain us (throughout every season). Intimacy with God is our form of security. Intimacy produces the confidence that we need to know that we can trust that the Father's plans for us will manifest, regardless of our circumstances.

Courtney

I met a young lady through a small group in the young adult ministry at my church. Yep, you guessed it—Courtney was her name. If I can, allow me to take a moment to describe this woman to you. Ms. Courtney was always glam. I mean from head-to-toe—glam. Hair, makeup, clothes—everything was fabulous! Courtney stands at about 5'6 and she has very dark African-American skin. She has the smoothest dark skin that you will ever see. She is small in frame, but her huge personality and fierce curly fro—or perfect twist out—give her a presence as large as a giant. Courtney is a makeup artist, so her makeup would always be on point, if she decided to wear it. Her eyebrows are a "snatch" level ten! She's just gorgeous.

One day as I was preparing to do a mime presentation, Courtney came into the restroom. She began speaking, and immediately, her presence commanded my full attention. "The Spirit of God is all over you," she said to me. "You have a very special anointing. You are so powerful in the Spirit, but I don't think you understand fully, just how powerful you really are." She continued by saying that God would do great and powerful things in my life.

We went into the service, but before we did, Courtney and I set a lunch date. Just like that, our friendship was formed.

She and I hung out often. She told me that God sent her into my life and that she was here to support me, no matter what… and I believed it. After a while, I started to realize that Courtney was always consistent. Make-up or no make-up, she always stood tall. Whether she wore heels or flats, she walked like a model, with her shoulders back and held high. Whether we did lunch at BJ's or Popeye's, (more often Popeye's for the two-piece special) she entered every restaurant as if *she* were the CEO. All of this while being so supportive, loving, and kind caused me to gravitate toward her and find inspiration that I did not know I needed. Courtney was humble and always willing to listen when I had problems. She openly shared how she found success in different areas, but she also respected my accomplishments, while providing me subtle pointers on how to be a better me.

As we grew closer and closer, I realized that I needed some of what Courtney had. I needed confidence, and lots of it. During this time, it became clear that confidence is a physical "thing." People believe that all spiritual things aren't physical, and that's not true. Courtney was the real thing. She was consistent. Her posture was strong and unwavering, yet still graceful. She was strong spiritually— and grounded in faith, and that strength manifested in the form of confidence.

One warm Sunday evening, she and I went to Chili's. I arrived to the restaurant before her. She didn't see me when she sashayed in the restaurant; I was sitting in the waiting area on the side. I watched her and her five-year-old daughter. She walked in with confidence and stood in that foyer like she was striking a pose at the end of the runway, but in the most natural way. Her posture was perfect. She looked around until she saw me. The way she carried herself, you would have thought we were at some five-star restaurant. I knew by her kindness that she was not arrogant, but it took me some time to process what was different about her. There were many weekends when we would go to Popeye's on Sundays and order the two-piece special. Courtney's mannerisms remained consistent. She never backed down. She never switched up. She was always that same—secure, steady, confident Courtney. We built each other up. My weaknesses were her strengths, and her weaknesses were my strengths. We were the perfect example of Proverbs 27:17, "As iron sharpens iron, so one person sharpens another."

Now of course by the time I noticed all of this, I realized Courtney had more going for herself than just outer beauty. Truthfully, I knew I could never be her and she could never be me. So I began to pray and ask God, that in my own way, for Him to give me what Courtney had—confidence! I said, "Lord I know I'm not Courtney. I don't desire to be her, but I want what she has with you, and I need YOU to give that to me directly. I want to be fully convinced of Your promises. Lord, when You tell me something, I want it to be enough for me. I want to stop second guessing my destiny and my greatness. I don't want to be afraid of my future anymore. I want the courage to stand in the manifestation of who You say I am, no matter who I am around."

After I prayed to the Lord about being confident, I began to search the Word for the biblical perspective on confidence.

During the time when I was gaining more biblical insight about confidence, I realized that I would often change my own behavior and mannerisms based on the people who were around and the environment that I was in.

One moment I would be secure in my purpose and the next moment, I acted like I didn't have a clue who God made me to be, and I needed validation. I was a double-minded "man" (James 1:8) in the flesh. It was as if I was pan-handling for a prophecy. I was behaving as if I needed some else to tell me who I was. I knew that God had showed me my future and His plan for my life, but years of rejection from people whom I respected as leaders in the faith caused me doubt what God said about me. Unconsciously, I turned my identity off and on at convenient times. I knew what I was doing, and yet I hated the fact that I allowed myself to turn "it" (my very own dose of confidence) on and off. I knew how to behave classy and when to show my class, but I also knew when and how to act "ghetto." I allowed whoever I was around to take me to whatever level they were on. If a person seemed like they would be intimidated by my anointing, or even my physical appearance, I would scale it down. When I was in a room filled with successful people, I would try to be secure in myself, but I felt intimidated by their successes. I always wondered if they could "read me" on sight and know that I was struggling financially or that I lacked the inner confidence that my smile and outer appearance showed. **I hated that.** *I wasn't leveling up to the promises that the Lord had given me. Instead, I was dumbing myself down to levels that I had long overcome.*

It didn't take long for me to begin feeling stuck in limbo, confused as to which version of me I should present to the public. At the time, I didn't believe that I was insecure, but I knew that I was not certain if I was truly who God said that I was, because at times it was hard to see the full picture of this amazing woman God declared me to be.

I have a friend name "Shayla," and she's what many people would define as "ghetto." She's loud, complacent, and unwilling to reach for more. She's been stuck at the same level in many areas of her life, for years, regardless of how often I tried to encourage her to do better. It got to a point where I could only spend time with her when I could relate to "the struggle." However, it became impossible. My life, calling, and physical needs required me to step things up. I could no longer be comfortable with the bad credit struggle, because I was making the changes necessary for me to get a new car.

I found myself pretending to be secure when I was around successful and affluent people. I would act like I was aware of my potential when I was surrounded by people of great influence. When it seemed fitting, I would lower the perspective I had of myself and my behavior would reflect insecurity every time the occasion seemed fitting. Most times, I would opt-out of confidence because I compared my success to others and felt I couldn't measure up—even though Hebrews 10:35-36 tells us not to do that because confidence has its reward!

I grew angry with myself the most when I turned off my confidence (my "It Factor") to be around certain people. I didn't like having to dumb myself down. Why couldn't I just be the confident person who I was in the kingdom? As I began to be in different environments, I became more aware of my personally shifts—my code-switching, and it was obvious that when I was around wealthy people working at the law firm or at banquets, I felt (and behaved) like the underdog.

As I mentioned earlier in this chapter, my lack of confidence was by design. For years, I was under attack from the enemy. Time after time, I was mishandled at the hands of people who were Intimidated by my gifts, my calling, and my success. Because I fell into agreement with the enemy, I lost battle after battle... Satan told me that I was inferior, weak, that I couldn't measure up to the attorneys or executives that were around, and that I had to instead "dumb down" my Godly beauty and power to fit into circles that God was trying to remove me from. I was a victim of rejection, manipulation, and spiritual abuse, and I was no longer operating in my victory that Jesus provided at the cross.

In the pages that follow, we're going to face the lies and deception head on, and you will learn how to release yourself from the bondage of religion and rejection to operate triumphantly with the confidence that God has bestowed upon you. Confidence is a real force that will determine the way you view yourself and how the world responds to you. It's time to go deep.

Chapter 2

The Breaking Point

Chapter Two: The Breaking Point

In the Beginning

Tread the deep waters of my life with me. My mother
is an apostle, and she's been in ministry for over twenty
years. She and I had a little rough patch. When I was
younger, when we lived Washington State, I was so young,
that her actions didn't seem like a problem to me. I just
knew I always wanted to be with my grandma all the time.
Things started to change in 2007, when our family was
suddenly uprooted. My immediate family at the time
consisted of myself, mom, my two younger brothers, and
two step siblings. Within a matter of thirty days, we went
from living a normal life with average day-to-day activities
in Washington State to moving to Dallas, Texas. It was
totally unexpected and we were headed to meet my
stepdad, who was already in Dallas. Shortly after we
arrived in Dallas, my mime ministry started to take off.
Whenever I had to take road trips to mime, my mother and
I enjoyed mother-daughter time. She and I became very
close. Churches gave us the finest treatment and the best
food. We flew everywhere, and each weekend, I looked

forward to a new adventure and exciting times with my mom. With the help of my mom, I was a teenager who ran a successful business, and everything pertaining to my mime career was flourishing from the ministry and business perspectives. I was making more money than I had ever seen. My mom and I were at a wonderful place in our relationship, as far as I could tell.

Allow me to backpedal for a quick moment. My mother got married when I was nine-years-old. Throughout the marriage, my mom and stepdad never saw eye-to-eye in quite a few areas. When I was nineteen, my stepdad told us that the Lord told him to divorce my mother and put us out. In the excruciating dry cold of January with that "revelation," he put me, my mom and two younger brothers out in the cold. As you could imagine, our lives were disrupted. My mother and I had no car and no emergency savings. My mom hadn't worked in over eight years, so there we were, with no savings, homeless, jobless, and carless. Friends in Washington sent cash for a rental car. We got a nice candy apple red Hyundai Sonata.

I found myself nineteen-years-old and suddenly thrust into grownup affairs. After we secured a rental car, my mom and I began our discrete operation, better known as operation move out of that house and into a new life without my stepfather. We had nowhere to put our houseful of belongings once he put us out, so I found a storage unit in Cedar Hill, Texas. Together, my mom and I loaded up the U-Haul truck I had rented and began the move. I was only 5'1 and about 120 pounds, but I knew that this was no time to be weak. My mom needed me, and as far as I was concerned, we were a team. As any good team player knows, there is no "I" in team. We stayed in the La Quinta Inn during our first two nights of being homeless. The La Quinta was fancy to me. My baby brother called it a "Hip-Hop Hotel" because it had flat screen televisions, a special breakfast buffet, a pool, and pizza (so he thought). The whole "divorce" thing seemed kind of fun at first. It almost felt like an upgrade! We worked that hotel. After we dropped my brothers off at school, my mom and I would go get extra bread, bagels, peanut butter and jelly from the breakfast bar, so we could have food to last us through the day. I was also fasting from meat at the time so I would get a couple of extra flour tortillas from Taco Cabana for twenty-five cents. This whole "divorce" ordeal almost felt like a joke to us. This feeling was perpetuated by so many incidents in the past. There had been many times before when my mom and her husband would get mad and act like they were breaking up. My mom would go through all the dramatics and make us pack our belongings. Of course this was annoying because we would always have to unpack within an hour or two. To my siblings and I, the game could be over any minute, and we could be back in our home.

That moment never came. I became accustomed to my new routine. I spent the days with my mom, while my brothers were at school. On one particular day, she pulled into the parking lot of a park and we took a nap. I felt so much peace sleeping in the front of that park, because there was no commotion around. We were away from my stepdad once in for all. That overwhelming feeling of peace remained during the time my mom and her husband were separated. I felt peace and uncertainty at the same time, and for some reason, I'd rather take that uncertainty if it meant I could remain in peace.

I was happy that they were divorced. Truth be told, our home never felt like a safe haven or a place for me. There was always tension and pressure to do everything right. There were so many limitations and unwritten rules. When they divorced, I felt free for the first time. Freedom seemed too big and too much to handle, but it also felt good. My step father was controlling and angry. We always had to walk on egg shells wondering how he felt on any given day.

After two days in the hotel, we stayed with my managers for my mime ministry. Remember, we were still in the dead of winter. One day, it froze and those icy streets and frost-bitten temperatures became our saving grace. We prayed to God every day that it would freeze again the next day so we could have time to figure out what we were going to do next. The roads stayed icy for two weeks straight and my managers let us stay with his family during that time. We were *beyond* grateful. So this two-week time period in the freezing cold was a blessing to us. I could focus on other things with the assurance that we'd have a place to lay our heads at night.

After leaving my manager's house, we were forced to move into a rundown hotel across the street. It was no longer fun and games. The hotel office smelled like smoke and urine; it was bad, but it was all we could afford. Drunkards and drug addicts roamed the area. Voices of those who never slept rang through the night, leaving little room for a good night's rest. I was scared to go from the car to our hotel room door without my mom watching me.

After the motel, we stayed at my mom's mentors house. They had trained us both in the ministry. While we were there, my mom left for a while, and said she was going to Washington State to check on the ministry that we'd left behind. She was still overseeing the pastor of that church. She stayed away longer than I had expected. I began to worry, and so I called and called, with no answer. Finally, one night she answered her phone and was whispering. I asked her if she was alright. She said yes, but she rushed me off the phone. The next day, I suspected something wasn't right. I went to my baby brother's school to visit him for lunch. I asked how he was doing and what had been going on with him, because he was staying and my soon-to-be ex step dad's house while my mom was out of town. Then my brother spilled the beans. He told me that my mom was at the old house staying with them! She had snuck away to go back to her supposed ex, and she left me and my other brother behind. I was so angry with her, and more so, crushed and heartbroken. I couldn't understand why she would abandon us to be with him. That was not the first time she had done it either, but it always seemed like she had to choose between him and us. This particular time, I was not sure if she was choosing on her own or if he was making her choose. But I noticed that she would rather be with him over us. My step dad made her feel like it was either him or us. If she was going to be with him, she had to leave her children behind. I was heartbroken when my baby brother told me mom had been at the house for a few days. Why would my mom lie about him? Why would she try to hide her relationship with him? Why would she lie to me? These were the questions that I had as a teenager forced into adulthood, and unfortunately, they were questions that did not come with easy answers.

Soon, my mom returned. She and my stepdad had apparently called it quits again and the divorce was still a go. Our broken family stayed at my spiritual father's house for about three months. After that, we finally moved into our own place. This entire time, I was in school online at Colorado Technical University. During this time, my mom never worked. She and I would take out loans. The loans kept us afloat. I also had mime contracts with the school district where I graduated, and my life's joy became teaching mime classes. At seventeen-years-old, I was the youngest contractor for the city. The mime income, massive student loan debt, food stamps, and help from family here and there supported us financially. This instability lasted from 2011 to 2013. During the entire two years of homelessness and unstable arrangements, my mother never clocked in to a 9 to 5.

Fast forward to the Spring of 2013. I looked in my mom's phone one day, and I saw a text that she sent to her ex-husband. It read, "I love you with all of my heart." That's when I put two and two together to figure out that they had been secretly dating.

By this time, my mom appointed me as pastor when I was twenty-years-old. She licensed me and set me in place the day after my birthday. Time passed, and one Sunday, my mom brought her ex to our church—the church that I led. My mom allowed him to come up to the front of the church and lay hands on me. In front of everyone in the congregation, this man said I had father issues and I needed to be healed. Of course I held it together in the moment. To save face, I allowed him to, "pray away my daddy issues"—that he contributed to [because I received him as a father]. When I got by myself, I flipped out.

The following week, my God-sister and I worked really hard to cook a nice dinner for our Easter meal. After

34

church, we went home, and shortly after, my mom's boyfriend-ex-husband showed up at the house. My mom tried to give him a special seat at the table. She wanted us to serve him and bring him "his" plate. At this point, I was pissed! I mean boiling. I was so heated that I could barely sit through grace, you hear me? This man was praying over our meal as if he was the head of the household or something. In my mind, all I could think was *mom are you kidding me? Did you not forget that this man who you expect us to honor is the same man who put us out in the cold, during the middle of winter, with no place to go?!* I could not deal with this situation, so I asked to be excused. Furious, I took my Easter dinner to my room, and began to plot out a plan of escape. I kept thinking to myself, *really mom? After all he did? Now you want us to serve him like some king?* I was livid. In that moment, I knew that I could no longer pastor that church, and more importantly, I could no longer serve under my mom's leadership. It just wouldn't work; too much had gone on and it was unhealthy. Especially if mess like that would continue. I finally had enough and I noticed the admiration I once had for my mom was fading rapidly.

Even though we moved into our own house, we struggled financially. One night, my mom and her ex-husband brought home pizza that he had apparently paid for unbeknownst to me. After we ate, my mom said, "Mr. K brought us pizza. You all should tell him thank you." I wanted to gag myself, throw that pizza back up, and hand it to him. And for the record, I hate throwing up. This man's presence made furious. I couldn't stand him coming to the house.

I was angry with my mom and I felt betrayed. During the divorce proceedings, (prior to them getting back together) my siblings and I talked to my mom about our feelings towards this man. My brothers exposed things that "Mr. K" and his kids had done and said to them. There were serious accusations of mistreatment and even bullying and abuse. Despite knowing all of that, my mother continued to see him.

As if the situation wasn't bad enough, my mom announced that on August 3, 2013, she and her ex-husband would remarry and recreate their wedding day. That was the game changer. I had done everything my mother had always asked me to do. I was always the angel child. Even to this day, she says that she could never remember me talking back to her. I would've have honestly followed my mom off a cliff. I was loyal to a fault. I remember her saying that "God said" for her to remarry her ex-husband. Any other time when she would say "God said," I believed her and eagerly followed suit. But that time, I just couldn't believe that God would actually instruct her to remarry a man that had done us so much harm. After being in a place of peace for the years while they were divorced, I just could not convince myself that this marriage was right. He was controlling and manipulative, and my mother was not the same, while under his influence. So for the first time, I "disagreed" with my mom, and voiced my opinions about this nonsense loud and clear and respectfully. She knew word-for-word, encounter after encounter, and reason upon reason, specifically why I did not want her to remarry him. I felt hurt, isolated, persecuted, and betrayed. My mom made a poor decision, but this time I couldn't just go along with it.

That was also the first time I ever entertained the thought that someone I considered a leader could be wrong. Any other time, I would have accepted whatever was handed to me, but not with that re-marriage business. My mom's marriage was the turning point that I needed to wake me up and open my eyes to the religious control and manipulation that I had been subjected to.

For the first time, I decided that I would not be controlled on any level! Not by my family and not in ministry. Of course my mom flipped the script on me. It was like she literally tried to make me look like the bad guy. She said I was in rebellion. I felt like I was the only level-headed one in the situation.

With the wedding quickly approaching, I knew I would have to make my exit from my mother's house, and quickly, once I was wide awake to the control and spiritual attacks that I was under. Unfortunately, God told me years before any of this took place to leave for college to attend CFNI, but I didn't obey. When the divorce happened, I convinced myself that I was the provider for my family, which was a space that only God could truly fill. I let other people convince me that following the dream God put in my heart was wrong. Honestly, this series of events was the only thing I can fathom that could have caused me to go back to relying on God to (fully) direct me.

The very person I drew back on my dreams to accommodate went and made a decision despite my inconvenience and left me lonely in my place of disobedience to God. Had I left years before, I never would have felt so bad. This process hurt me, because I never stepped out on other things God told me to do. Don't worry the story gets better. I'm thankful that because of God's grace, what could have been a break down started my break through.

There were a few steps I took to overcome manipulation and an unhealthy environment:

First, I had to get my physical self out of the situation. I stepped down from being pastor and let my mom know that I would no longer be a part of her church. I joined my spiritual father's church to take some time to heal. I knew that getting my head right would be an intensive process. For the first two weeks after I stepped down from my pastoral position, I stayed with a minister from my new church home. She stayed smack dab in the middle of the hood. I remember thinking to myself, *if my mom ever finds out where I am staying, she is going to laugh her head off because I am over here in "struggle land."* It wasn't like my family was living the crème de la crème, but we were in a decent neighborhood. Although there were drug addicts and thugs surrounding the new place where I was staying, this would be the place where I cried out to the Lord from the depths of me. I danced before the Lord on my first night there, and wept so hard that I couldn't breathe. While it served its purpose, I knew that this was only a temporary dwelling. The minister ended up calling my mom and telling her where I was staying, even after I asked her not to.

This situation was a huge lesson for me. Sometimes, when we leave toxic situations, our next stop may not be a bed of roses. Instead, we find ourselves in transition places—places that allow us to reflect and cry out to God. Places that provide peace in the midst of trials.

Chapter 3
The Start of Transition

Chapter Three: The Start of Transition

If I didn't know in my spirit who I was supposed to be and that I was God's prophet, had I listened to what everyone else was saying, I would have *gone astray from God* like so many others before me. In fact, I was close to gone. Right before I stepped down as pastor of my mom's church and moved out of her house, I was in my room packing to leave for CFNI. My head had never felt so clouded and stuffed with attacks on my mind. My mind was literally filled up *with mess.* I was getting ready for work early one morning, and I turned on YouTube to search for sermons to encourage myself. That's when I found Cindy Jacobs. She started prophesying on the coming year. She prophesied miracles, and without laying hands, people were being healed. Congregants who had visible physical disabilities and pain literally leaped out of their seats and started running in various directions around the church as a result of their manifested physical healings. That was the first time I saw even a glimmer of my assignment in the spiritual realm.

That Cindy Jacobs moment gave me the gust of "fight" that I *needed* to leave my mother's house, confident that God was with me for the journey ahead. My breakout wouldn't be easy though. It seemed like my mom came up against me every day that followed with another spiritual attack. She conjured up drama because I did not agree with her marriage. One day, I was feeling a little nervous about stepping out on my own because, mind you, I had never done anything without my mom's approval, let alone contrary to her opinion! One afternoon, I sat on the stair case and she stood at the bottom of the stairs. I asked her, "Mom if something happens, can I come back home?" She literally started cracking up laughing right in my face. You would've thought someone took her to a comedy show the way she hurled out that gut-rooted laughter. And to top it off, she called my little brother over to laugh with her. It was the ultimate mockery, and that's when I knew it was on! To be honest, sometimes I can't believe this stuff happened to me. It was nothing but the Lord who sustained me!

My next major move was enrolling into Christ for the Nations Institute (affectionately known as CFNI), which would turn out to be one of the best experiences of my life. Once I got to CFNI, my healing truly began. This school is a bible college that focuses on international relations. The culture of the school, for me, was a refresher— free, with a relaxed dress code, and everyone was on fire for God. Many of the school's leaders were Caucasian, and the way they did life and ministry were completely foreign to me. This was where I got a clean slate with God. I was completely wiped clean of all the routines and the bondage I had experienced before. I got rid of faulty thoughts that had shaped my world view. This place forced me to confront everything that I had been taught and question it. I realized God was not intimidated by my questions, because He has all the answers. I constantly reminded myself that I could not look backwards and I had to have zero tolerance for manipulation. Being on the CFNI campus was a much-needed breath of fresh air.

Many of the black people I knew in ministry were very discouraging of my decision to attend CFNI. They said things like, "You don't have to go to school to be anointed. You don't have to pay all that money to learn the Word." In my heart, I knew I wasn't going to CFNI to validate my anointing, but I also knew that I needed to invest in training from people I could maintain healthy Godly relationships with. I realized their words were just another form of manipulation and their justification for not supporting, even after they had previously promised that they'd be there.

"Anything you need daughter," so many of them had said.

After leaving for CFNI with contention from my "family," my mom unfortunately, who was my biggest opposition at the time, aired our business to my connections from the mime ministry and business. She told people that I "left her," "ran away," "was in rebellion and being rude," and "Majisty has father issues." I wanted to keep things to myself, and her behavior during this time made me feel more betrayed and alone. I didn't feel I could win with any option. I ended up taking the hit and swallowing my pride. Next, just as I anticipated, pastors and leaders rejected me, ignored me, and almost completely stopped calling for my ministry once they were under the impression that I was in rebellion.

Christ for the Nations was really the place where I started heal. It really tore down the veil of religion, and by "religion" I mean the set of rules that Christians tend to follow that have little or nothing to do with how close to God they become. The religious spirit is usually accompanied by manipulation. There was freedom and liberty all around, from how the people at CFNI dressed to their style of worship.

The Word that Changed It All

One of the most precious truths the Lord showed me was that *He was not who 'they' said He was*. I could hear God petitioning me and crying out because He wanted to truly show Himself to me. The Father wanted to show me that He was not rejecting me like others did and that He was not angry with me. Do you recall in the gospels when Jesus asked the disciples, "Who do men say that I am?" What people said about Jesus was different than the truth, a truth that Peter actually knew! How we perceive God has a great effect on our relationships with Him. Within the church, many people are abused because of leaders who have the wrong impression about God and consequently pass those misperceptions down to their congregations. We have people who feel qualified to lead simply because they have a "relationship" with God. However, I submit to you that in this hour God is calling for His bride to have more than *just* a relationship with Him. He's calling all of us to have intimacy with Him and know Him deeply. This call is not just for leaders, but for everyone! The church, which is the bride of Christ, has become content with having a relationship with God and no intimacy whatsoever. I remember the Lord spoke to me one day. He said, *"Majisty, I will always love you. There is nothing you can do to make me love you any more or any less. No matter where you go, no matter what you do, I will always love you. But if you want intimacy, that's in the consistent coming [to seek me]."*

The truth is that God's love for us will never change. But we must not stop at love; we must desire to be intimate with Him. We must create a space of vulnerability with God and make that our dwelling place. Pursuing intimacy with God presents a challenge for many people, because we've become conditioned to making our interaction with God based on what we can get from Him, without even knowing that's what we've done. The worst part about this is that we're immune to the effects this selfish approach has on our relationships with God. In fact, we think it's okay because we think God is only trying to get something out of us! Specifically, what I mean is that we *only* think God wants to "use" us. Think about it. How many times have you heard a church leader say, "God wants to use you?" We hear it so often that we find no fault in that way of thinking. While it is true that we are the Master's vessels, sometimes we get the wrong connotation. We are also

God's children and His friends as the scriptures mention many times. I believe that a part of our duty as believers is to sit with God in places of authority. As I write that, I'm reminded of the scripture Ephesians 2:5-6 "even when we were dead in trespasses, made us alive together with Christ (by grace you have been saved), and raised *us* up together, and made *us* sit together in the heavenly *places* in Christ Jesus…" God didn't create us "in His image" to be mere robots, slaves, or weaklings without authority. We were created with dominion, designed to rule over the earth. In order to do this, we must sit with God, commune with Him, and hear from Him. In other words, intimacy is required to evolve into who He wants us to be.

I remember the Lord revealing the concerns of His heart to me one day. He said Majisty, "I have no one to sit with." As I reflected on my days as a loner in grade school, I sympathized with how He felt. What the Lord was showing me is that members in the body of Christ are not willing to be still long enough to commune with God in places of authority. As you go deeper in God, the matters of God's heart and not just His hand, will have to become priority to you. Do the things on God's heart matter to you? Are you watching His gaze? Or is your prayer time only about you?

At CFNI, I learned simple truths (like the above) that were all new to me, and I was also confirmed in my gifts. For instance, I had always been accustomed to operating in the supernatural; none of those things ever seemed strange to me. But in the environment where I grew up, my power in the spirit was being quenched because basic kingdom principles like integrity, kindness, love, compassion, and stewardship took a back seat. What was happening to me in the spirit reminded me of what happened in the natural pertaining to my education. When I was a kid in kindergarten, I had very strong reading and comprehension skills. When I left private school to attend public school, I went through testing. I tested well enough to skip the first grade. Any challenges that I had with math or other subjects were quickly resolved as long as my teachers could provide me with curriculum to read. While my comprehension was strong, I struggled a little bit with grammar, because I missed all of the first grade lessons. I had challenges with punctuation. I found myself advanced in one area, but playing catch-up in this other area that was so vital. Similarly, my spiritual environment was not void of miracles and prophecies, but I was surrounded by people who did not know how to steward one another. Quite frankly, it seemed like they didn't care. They valued prophecy over love, and 'money miracles' over diligence and stewardship. They would rarely just call on people to see how they were doing. With a unique view of being inside the church with an outsider's perspective, and a keen ear to the heart of God, I learned that He was concerned with my relationship with Him, above everything else. Growing up as a pastor's kid, the priority was always ministry, ministry, ministry! At CFNI, I learned principles like Christians are to be good stewards over our family at home, before the ministry. But this was not what I saw demonstrated in my home.

I really believe that my experience at CFNI was a divine interception to save me from becoming the "church girl gone wild." I honestly believe that there are so many *Church Girls Gone Wild,* because the religious rules have been nailed into their hearts, while the importance of creating a loving relationship with our Father has been forsaken. The religious spirit uses fear to invoke holy behavior, which quickly fades. It is our love for God that should draw us to live holy lifestyles. When hard times hit, these so-called wild church girls lack the direct relationship with God that will sustain them through life's storms.

Sometimes demonic spirits are embedded so deeply within Christians that they cannot see that they are no longer behaving like Christ. I knew I would have to fight.

Learning New Things

Christ for the Nations taught me other important principles like it was okay to get a job outside of the church and work "in the world" to sustain myself. I know that sounds foreign *and basic,* but by the time I got to the bible college campus, I thought that secular employment meant I didn't have faith for my ministry to flourish. I heard misconceptions like "Adam's work was cursed." As if Christ didn't redeem us from *every* curse of the law! I was always frustrated by that notion, because it caused my family to struggle unnecessarily. We went through seasons where we couldn't afford to turn on the heat in the Texas winter, or had limited groceries, and nowhere to go. Some nights, when I would mime, the church ladies would fix us a "church plate" to go and that was the only way my brothers ate.

During her divorce, my mom acted like the rent was a national crisis every month. I always felt this undue pressure to always be in ministry and never to get a job, because of the faulty teachings I'd been persuaded to believe: *if I get a job, that means I do not trust God for my ministry to "take off."* Ugh…just ugh!

Dean Foxxi at CFNI stepped in as a mentor figure and made a major impact on my life. She always had time to listen and speak wisdom into my life. I remember one day I was stressed out about whether or not the Lord wanted me to work. She simply said, "Majisty, if you have steady bills, you need steady pay." She also hit me with an obvious yet foreign truth, "The Lord will be with you wherever you go." She had to remind me of that, because I had heard so many lies that God would not be with me if I left my certain ministries or turned down opportunities. Her words of wisdom helped me break through lies that were told to me by people who operated in witchcraft within the church.

Our worship experiences were free at CFNI. Our unrestricted environment set the stage for Holy Spirit to flow. I had my own encounters with the Lord. I experienced music that I had never heard and sang words to the Lord that sounded so beautiful. This was the first time that I experienced God like this. I remember being in a balcony during worship, and I could hear the Lord crying out to me in a desperate tone. And He was saying, *"I'M NOT HIM. I'M NOT HIM."* And as I briefly mentioned earlier, the Lord was showing and telling me that He wasn't who others said He was. He was not the angry God waiting for me to fail, so He could punish me type-of-God that had been presented to me. While at CFNI, in that pure and anointed environment, I saw the truth for what it was. If you have ever experienced control and manipulation in religious environments, you know that anytime you come up with a thought or a plan that does not fit a personal agenda, a leader will say that God is not pleased with it. I started working, very hard, to say the least.

I noticed that having my own money broke the financial dependency I had on my family. To a certain extent, I felt that as long as I needed my family's money, it seemed like they felt they had the right to control me simply because they would send me money here and there. This embedded a deep feeling inside that God was mad at me, and I soon realized that it was all a lie. All of these false notions about God and layers of bondage were removed. Bible school was the place where both my mind and body broke free. I overcame the attacks of control and manipulation.

Pursuit of Freedom

My deliverance was rooted in the truth that God loved me and God liked me. I had to believe God's truth, because I was accustomed to the move of God in me being stifled by people who didn't enjoy my creativity.

You too can break free from this bondage. There are two parts of control: the controller and the controlee (person who is being controlled). Each party has their own equal role. I had to take ownership of my part and rid myself from allowing control and the victim mentality that came with it. I had to move beyond the belief that there always needed to be someone other than Jesus to help me access God. In other words, I thought I needed a mediator between me and God. The enemy had me believing his lies. I wrestled with the question, "Can God say something to me, even if other people don't approve of what He's saying?" So I was in a fight to hear God for myself because, I was in a place of not even believing that God could speak to me unless I had someone else to "okay" it.

This was spiritual manipulation and control at its best. I also realized that I had the spirit of religion in me, because I felt the *need* to put another mediator in place. In my case, the mediator that I felt I needed was my mom, who was also my pastor. I learned that there is only one mediator— the only filter for your prayer life is the Lord Jesus Christ. This doesn't mean you don't need leadership or need to be submitted. I believe in accountability and taking the Word before two and three witnesses, but for me it had gone to an unhealthy place. *I had to get pass that!*

Identity Rehab

Bible College gave me the tools to get through what I call a "spiritual rehabilitation process" with the Lord. One of the most important tools and steps to rehabilitation was professional counseling. Professional, as in not from family members. Not venting to my home girls—real, legit, certified counseling. I went to professional counseling at my new home church, and that was amazing! It was good to have a healthy neutral party to talk and listen to. Finally, there was someone who didn't have some hidden agenda against me. My counselor told me that she could see I had been accustomed to being in environments that stifled me. She said, "By the time we're done, you're going to get your wings because it's time for you to soar and be okay with growing and doing well."

Another step the Lord had me take towards confidence was journaling. I journaled often to teach myself to appreciate my own thoughts. I wanted to see how my mindset was changing over time and notice any paradigm shifts within myself. I also needed to log the things that the Lord was telling me to bring me out of the isolated space I was in because of how I was persecuted. I also found it refreshing to express what I was feeling without being concerned with how someone else would respond. Have you ever told someone something that you were happy about and their response and level of excitement did not match yours? Or have you ever had a great idea or a perspective on something and decided to share with someone you trusted, who responded by telling you how *you* think? I loved journaling because I never had to worry about other people's responses to my mind's treasures. Journaling allowed me the private opportunity to value my own thoughts, revelations, and moments with God and cherish them in my heart. I was also able to process decisions and issues in a clear way.

To overcome the attacks meant that I had to cut off people who were trying to control me. Initially, I had to go through a stint of time where I would only answer the phone for certain people just to be sure they were okay. As I got stronger, I was able to revisit the boundaries of when and how I dealt with those people. And you may be able to apply this in your own life. Perhaps you shouldn't discuss ministry with some people in your life. There may be others with whom you do not discuss your finances or your love relationship. And no matter who you are, there are some people in your circle that do not need to know your failures and challenges, especially if they don't believe what God has told you anyway. When people don't believe what God has spoken to you, do not get frustrated. They don't understand because it's not their assignment. If your revelation was meant for them to understand, God would have told them directly, but He didn't. He told you, and that has to become enough for you.

And during this life-changing point in my life when the pain from religion had pressed down on my shoulders like a heavy weight, the Lord showed me that He wants the depths of our hearts to be exposed to Him. Intercourse is only one facet of intimacy. So when it comes to spiritual growth, we absolutely should read our bible, pray, fast, and go to church—those basic things the Bible tells us to do, but we can't stop there. We must spend vulnerable time with God. We must become intimate with God by exposing ourselves to Him completely.

I had been in church my entire life, and the religious spirit clutched me tightly. That spirit destroyed me, and it was the Lord who had to build me back up and restore me. I had to get to know Him for myself. That same knowing that Adam and Eve had— not the intercourse part but that intimate knowing on a soul and spiritual level—that knowing is a place where He knows the depths of me and I desire to know the depths of Him. I went through severe loneliness. The Lord took me back to this place where it was like all I could see was the real Him and that's what saved me. It was as if I had to get saved all over again, because I was in a system—a stronghold. I was with the Lord, but somewhere along the way, I got caught up in the ministry hype and the preaching hype.

Get prepared, When you get ready to break free from control into confidence or, more specifically, from religion into revival, some of the people you love will likely turn their backs on you if they are not secure in who they are.

You have to get secure with God, and He must become your best friend if you are going to make it through that time.

Chapter 4

Identity Rehab:

Who Am I(Really)?

Chapter Four: Identity Rehab-Who Am I (Really)?

I started preaching at the age of ten-years-old. Growing up, I always had an awareness of the presence of the Lord. I had an encounter with the Lord at "an early age" you could say. I remember being filled with the Holy Spirit with the evidence of speaking in tongues at the age of eight-years-old. I would read the bible and pray for hours as a kid without anyone having to tell me to. I set out on a mission to be God's best friend.

Some people were encouraged and inspired by what God was doing in my life and others weren't. Jealous people tried to discredit my testimony by saying, "Oh you ain't neva been through nothing. You can't tell me nothing." It left me feeling stuck between a rock and a hard place. On one hand, people discouraged me from engaging in sinful behaviors and going wild. On the other, since I had never smoke, drank alcohol, or had sex, people acted like I was unfit to preach the gospel. Now isn't that a doozy? The fact of the matter is that God is who He is regardless of our circumstances. He's Jehovah Rapha (the Lord that Heals) whether a person's cancer is in remission or they were recently diagnosed. He is Jehovah Jireh (God that Provides) whether you're a millionaire or homeless, jobless, and carless. There's a theology in today's Christian circles that says you need to go through something (hard) for God do something or be God. That kind of thinking comes from the fault of people thinking that they can determine who God is by looking at their circumstances. It should be the other way around. You can determine your circumstances by looking at who God is! **I chose to stand on the Word of the Lord and the convictions that God gave *me*.** My mom encouraged me not to buckle to the pressure of having to "go get a testimony." She said, God is great no matter what your story is. Just because you may not have to call on Him in the way that some others do (or did) it does not mean there is weakness or fault in your relationship with God. The Word of God is true and the scriptures are our foundation. Regardless of your background, take no shame in declaring the Word of God. What I'm trying to say is to be content with who you are. Walk in who God called you to be. Don't be complacent, but know that standing in your God-given identity is the best way to get the harvest that belongs to you. And when God has given you an assignment, don't just shuck it off in your heart by saying, "Oh someone else can minister to those people. Someone else can answer that call." God called you for a reason.

When I cut off critical, toxic, and complacent people to seek out the real me, my spiritual leadership told me that I would never make it without them. It rocked my world, and I literally forgot everything that I believed about myself and I forgot what God said about me. God had to tell me who I was *again*.

True Story: I needed a letter of recommendation for a scholarship. One of the people I asked for the letter recommended that I write the letter and they sign it. I found myself procrastinating, even though I knew that the deadline for the letter was coming up very quickly. I couldn't figure out why I was delaying something that I knew was time sensitive and so important. One day, I finally sat down to write the letter. I wrote, "Majisty is…" and for the longest time, I could not get past those words, "Majisty is." All that came to my mind was the accusations that had been spoken over me by people who didn't understand my situation over the past few years. As I filled in the blank in my mind, I heard the words people had been speaking against me so loudly. "Majisty is…rebellious. She's just bitter. She'll never make it. She's young and stupid. She doesn't know what she's doing. She's wearing that nappy hair." I broke down crying, in that very moment, because I realized that the negative thoughts from others towards me had begun to sound like my own. It had been going on for so long that I couldn't tell the difference within myself between "their" accusations and my perception of myself. I cried because I believed what they had said about me. I cried, not because I was frustrated with myself about believing something untrue. I cried in self-pity, because I was convinced that what they said was true. It was almost as if in that moment that God was letting me know that He would pick me up and dust me off.

That night when I got home, I wrote down every ill word I had heard about myself over the previous two to three years. I allowed myself to grieve over those accusations, and then the Lord came in and gave me His truth. He began to show me that just because others didn't know what I was doing, it did not mean that He didn't know what *He was doing.* The Lord gave me multiple truths to speak over myself, and He commanded me to look at them and say them in the mirror every morning and night. I would wake up and say things like, "Majisty, I give you permission to grow today. I am happy. I am kind. I care about myself, and it's okay to care about myself. I love myself. God is for me. God is with me. I will not fear." The Lord also lead me to scriptures that encouraged me and helped me not to fear. As I would do these exercises every day, the Lord guided me into a posture of confidence. I no longer walked around insecure. At one point, I self-consciously thought that the new people in my life would agree with my accusers. Once God changed my thinking about me, I stopped this, and I could see myself changing. I dressed better, smiled more, grew unafraid to socialize, and I tried new things.

Day-by-day, the Lord eliminated the lies I believed about myself and blessed me with His truth. I realized— because God confirmed—that I was never wrong for leaving home. I was strong enough to have my own mind, my own free will, and I chose God's best decision for me. The decision to leave home and step down as pastor only felt bad, not because I was making the wrong choice, but because I was one of few who were willing to leave everything that people glorify (titles) to make the right choice. I was rejected by others who were jealous because they didn't have the courage to make the choice that I had made.

I want you to recognize that you are enough. Your testimony is enough. So many times we pray to have other people's blessing. We see something that others have, and we ask God for the same thing. We see someone with a bold anointing, not realizing that it may work for them, but the Lord may have given you a gentle approach to handling people. The way you are works for the people He has called you to. Walk in the will of the Lord for your life—be you. If you are pretending to be someone else because you like what they have going on, it is as if you're sending mixed signals to heaven on who to bless—do you want Him to bless you or the person you're pretending to be?

Chapter 5
Beyond Relationship

Chapter Five: Beyond Relationship

Recognize that when religious spirits control and manipulate, what they speak sounds like something God would say. They prey on your pure desire to seek God. It sounds so close to "the truth" that you feel confused or wrong for even questioning it. Red flags for control and manipulation may include:

- a lack of respect for your thinking process
- comments like "This is the only real church. No one will treat you better than 'we' do."
- excessive managing of personal life details
- constant accusations of people being in rebellion or disobedient
- being divided from the masses or the leaders, even when you mean well.

For me, a part of coming out of the religious stronghold meant that I had to meet the Lord in a new way. During one of these intimate encounters, the Lord spoke to me and said, "Religion is the greatest enemy of revival." I realized that the stronghold that was opposed to my "revival" was the 21st century version of the Sadducccs and the Pharisees from the New Testament. Religion twists the Word of God in a way that He never meant it to be. These people twist the scriptures because they're not interpreting the Word through the context of relationship or intimacy with God. I remember Jesus speaking to me in such a compassionate way. He said, "I know what it was like for people to attack your calling because of their lack of understanding of the Father's words. They did it to me too." God reminded me of how people refused to believe in miracles and His supernatural power as if He had lost His touch. Religion attacked me and made me think that God was angry with me. I felt my ministry had been stripped and my success was a thing of the past. I overcame by coming to a place of intimacy with God and learning how intimacy is the opposite of religion. To be intimate with the Lord, make yourself vulnerable to God. He already knows the truth, but it is better when you go to Him willingly and honestly.

God showed me something that illustrated this point. A man can have no-strings-attached sex with a woman. He doesn't have to be physically attracted to the woman, and he does not need any type of additional incentives to have sex with her. After it's done, he can shake it off and not think twice about this sexual encounter the day after, after he has received what he wanted. (For women, not so much.) This is called intercourse, which is the actual act of having sex. But when a man is *intimate* with a woman, he becomes vulnerable to her. In that place of vulnerability, he grows sensitive to her needs and shares his secrets with her in a way that he wouldn't with anyone else. *Intimacy* is a spiritual and emotional experience. The Lord told me, "I'm ready for intimacy with my bride." He said, "My people come to church for intercourse!" We come to church and we look good doing it, and by the time we get to the parking lot, we shake off the service like nothing ever happened. Worship is going on and we don't expose our hearts, minds, and emotions to God. We allow people to drain our emotions to the point where we don't have anything left for God. We don't even allow ourselves to be changed. Spiritual intercourse is not enough for God these days.

Intimacy with God breeds holiness. The deeper I desire to go in Him, additional shackles of sin begin to fall off. As I draw closer to Him, the bondage of sin can no longer remain. I realize that I can only have one Lover, and I choose Him! Many people don't want God; they want what they can get out of God. And most people do not believe that God wants them, they think God wants something from them. Here's what I mean. People don't want God; they want what's in His hand. They chase healing or they chase prosperity, and they feel that God is just the most effective means to that end desire. There is nothing wrong with prosperity, but you must desire Him more than you want material things. Money cannot be your God.

On the other end of the spectrum, people think that this paradigm is okay because they think God does not want them. They think He only wants something from them. So many people carry themselves with the mindset of *God does not want me, He wants my sin or He wants my money.* Imagine it this way. I say, "Come to me." And instead, you decide to toss me your coat, your shoes, your watch, your belt, and you continue to stand at a distance. I wouldn't be satisfied with that, because I want "you." It's the same way with God. If you hand Him your tithes, your offering, your stress, your cares, you fast occasionally, you hand Him a couple of your sins—you may even stay celibate for a while, but all the while you never avail yourself fully to Him. God wants you not what you have. As you draw nigh to His presence, the bondage of sin falls off. God wants you and will draw all of you in.

Reconsidering Your Approach in Prayer

When I prayed, my natural inclination was to start out asking for forgiveness of my sins because I thought God saw me as a sinner. I would start out thanking God and then repent for my sins and continue from there in some sporadic manner. But that is not at all what the Bible tells us to do. I always said my 'thank you's' to the Lord and wanted to hurry up and repent for my sins so that God could hear me. An ineffective strategy to start a conversation with the Father is talking about sins that He has already forgiven.

Psalm 100:4 says, "Enter into His gates with Thanksgiving, and into His courts with praise. Be thankful to Him, and bless His name." Before anything, we should always come to God in a spirit of praise and giving Him thanks.

Matthew 6:9 is the model prayer. Let's take some ques from how Jesus prayed to apply to our own lives.

Verse 9: This, then, is how you should pray: "Our Father in heaven, hallowed be your name,

- We must acknowledge who God is.

Verse 10: your kingdom come, your will be done on earth as it is in heaven.

- Focus your efforts on learning what is on the Kingdom agenda for being established in the earth.

Verse 11: Give us today our daily bread.

- Request the necessary provision you need from God.

Verse 12: And forgive us our debts, as we also have forgiven our debtors.

- Ask God to forgive you for your wrongdoings and forgive others who have wronged you as well.

Verse 13: And lead us not into temptation, but deliver us from the evil one.

- We must honor God again.

Moving Out of a Negative Self Image

Colossians 2:23 says, "These things indeed have an appearance of wisdom in self-imposed religion, false humility, and neglect of the body, but are of no value against the indulgence of the flesh."

When the Apostle Paul wrote "these things," he was referring to the acts that people conduct to work as a set of their own commandments and acts of Gnosticism-which is self-punishment to acquire holiness. Paul called this behavior "the doctrine of man." He said that "man" looks on the outside as if their works are done in wisdom, but truly these works are the influence of a self-imposed religion. This type of behavior that Paul spoke of were not directions from God, and so they fell right in line with false humility and added no value when it came to walking in the true ways of the Lord.

Many people are afraid to walk in confidence, because they think in repetitive cycles of failure like, "What goes up must come down," and "All good things must come to an end." They carry a 'good times won't last long' type of mentality. Allow me to remind you that because we serve a mighty God and He is a Good Father, we have a right to walk in confidence, if for no other reason than because of who God is. People often resist confidence because they are afraid of failure or they think that to be confident, they have to be perfectly established or perfect all together. I'm reminded of a passage that affirms to me that I can count on the Lord as my safety blanket. In the bible, 2 Thessalonians 3:3-5 says, "But the Lord is faithful. He will establish you and guard you against the evil one. And we have confidence in the Lord about you, that you are doing and will do the things that we command. May the Lord direct your hearts to the love of God and to the steadfastness of

Christ." (ESV) Did you hear that? As Paul, Silvanus, and Timothy were writing to the church of Thessalonica, they expressed their own confidence in God about how well the church was doing at the time and their future pertaining to the things they had been instructed to do. That means we can trust God to establish us and trust Him to be effective regarding our own God-given assignments. We are a part of God's plan, so if we trust that all the factors of His plan will work, we have to believe in ourselves too! We are the vehicles that carry out the assignments from God. You should trust that God knew what He was doing when he saved you and when He called you. Do you believe what God said about you? Do you know what He spoke over you? It's time to believe God to a point of confidence. Be sure of yourself because God is with you!

In my own walk, every step that I made was a step toward destiny in faith. I had nothing ready to start living on my own. Stepping out to attend and move to the campus of CFNI was one of my biggest steps of faith. The school does not accept financial aid, and I applied to attend with no savings. I only had about three weeks to prepare. I needed a new car, tuition, and everything in between.

Anything that I was believing God for, the Lord was going to have to do it. I didn't know how things would fall in place for me, but I applied to CFNI and got approved for a full tuition scholarship to pay for my first semester. I did not learn of that until two or three days before I moved out of my mom's house. However, the lesson here is that when we take one step of faith, God has already done the rest.

When I enrolled into CFNI, my plan was to be there for three years. My spiritual father prophesied that I was supposed to be there for two. After a year and a half, I didn't have the money to finish. I couldn't reregister, so I had to move out. I couldn't go home. During this time, I worked an event—a share-a-thon that Daystar Television hosted for two weeks (this was similar to a telethon). There I met an aspiring pastor name John. He learned about my situation and asked a member of his church to let me stay with her. I didn't know her at all—she was a complete stranger. Yet, the Lord lifted her up to help me. I only knew Pastor John for two weeks. I didn't know this lady. I moved out to Weatherford, Texas, a place where I had never been, until it was time to live there.

She (Cindy) came, and she helped me pick up my stuff. I had been praying and was asking the Lord for confirmation that this faith move was also ordained by God. That day, I remember thinking to myself, *I really want a California pizza and a Coca-Cola from Chili's.* When Cindy came to get me, she asked me if I wanted to go to dinner. I asked her where she wanted to go. And she said, "I think I saw a Chili's on the way here." Even though it may sound silly, that was confirmation. She spoke what I held in the privacy of my thoughts. Only the Lord knew what was on my mind because I never told anyone. I felt that it was the Lord's way of saying, "I'm protecting you; I'm guiding you; I'm with you." This season of my life, although a blessing, was one of the toughest because by that time, I stepped out on faith and I really felt like I had failed. People laughed at me. Bible school wasn't finished. Now, I *felt* stuck, not to mention, every day I had a one hour commute each way between Weatherford and Dallas. One day, while taking that long haul, my car quit on me in the middle of the road. Pastor John had to come pick me up. Having no car immediately meant no job, but I was still thankful.

I knew God was going to use me to speak to the nations and show the world that He loves me. I had to still believe. I was homeless, carless, and jobless. *Yet I believed.*

Even in the times when I failed, I questioned *did I still hear the Lord say what I thought He said?* And that's when I learned that this is how the enemy works—like when he came to Eve and tempted her, saying, "Did you really hear God say that?" I still had to believe the consistency of the Word of God. I learned that we shouldn't go get a new plan when it looks like the Word of God isn't going to come through. You stick with the plan, and that's when the situation will come into alignment with what God spoke.

At this point in the journey, confidence really has to come into play, because by then, that's when your own thoughts or others around you, will begin to plant doubt such as, 'Oh you heard God say this, but it doesn't look like it?' I had to stand on my promise. *God still said I'm going to finish bible school, and God still said XYZ.* That's when I had to go back to His promises to me, and I realized that I didn't miss God. There were things going on behind the scenes that I couldn't see and people weren't doing what they were supposed to do.

Satan tried to tempt Jesus in Matthew 4:6, "If you are the Son of God," he said "throw yourself down. For it is written: "He will command his angels concerning you, and they will lift you up in their hands, so that you will not strike your foot against a stone." Take a moment to realize what Satan was doing. Satan was trying to get Jesus to prove His [Jesus'] identity to him [Satan], and Satan used the scriptures to tempt Jesus. A religious and manipulative spirit will always try to twist the scriptures and make you feel obligated to prove yourself. If Jesus overcame, so can you! If you have found yourself in a situation like Jesus was when He was tempted, remember that you have NOTHING to prove. NOTHING! By the time Jesus was tempted, God had already defined Jesus and announced their relationship to the world. This took place prior to Jesus going into the wilderness, during His baptism, when the Holy Spirit descended on Jesus like a dove and God said, "This is my beloved Son in whom I am well pleased." Spirits of religion and manipulation will try to force you to go over matters that have already been resolved!

Can I tell you that God knows who you are? He has a well-written plan for your life that cannot be stopped by any interference. God is the one who will announce who you are to the world. He will let the enemy, the church, and the world know that you are His child! The Lord takes care of His children. Let this be the last day that you run around in circles like you have a point to prove.

Next, we need to address that fact that when Satan speaks, he speaks lies from his own resources. The devil is a liar and nothing he says is true! Say that aloud right where you are! The devil is a liar and nothing he says is true! Even when Satan tried to speak the scripture; it was a lie because of who it was coming from. Have you ever wanted to believe what someone was saying, but you couldn't accept it as truth because of who it was coming from? Same way with the devil. When Satan said "if" it made everything that was proceeding from his mouth after become a lie. See because there are no 'ifs' in the Spirit. God does not make suggestions to his children. He gives us commands. The Word of the Lord is yes and amen! If that sentence (in the scripture) didn't have an "if" in it; it would've read, "You are the son of god. Throw yourself down." Which isn't even a compatible command for who Jesus is.

Without the "if" Satan would have:

1. Acknowledged God by saying "You are the Son of God."
2. Declared who God is.
3. Attempted to command Jesus to do something, which is beyond Satan's scope of authority.

4. Exposed the fact that he did not have the power to tell Jesus what to do.

The devil would love to try and put an "if" in your mind. He wants to make you question if you are who God said you are, just like he tried to do with Jesus. The devil has no new tricks. When circumstances come into what God has told you, the devil tries to put an "if" in your mind. The devil will also try to twist the intention with which prophetic words were given. Resist the temptation to believe that God's intentions are anything less than to dwell with you and prosper you.

I can hardly remember a time when I've had every resource financially and labor-wise all in line before I set out to do something. I knew it would take faith to go after my new kind of normal. So many people turned against me until it was just me and God, and that had to be enough. Instead of looking at the people who left me, I had to fix my eyes on God and be thankful for the people who stayed. I watched the Lord send people at many times on a day-to-day basis to help me with needs, words, and sometimes just hugs.

Do you know why confidence is so important? I stress confidence because it is an expression of your God-given authority. So many times, I hear people say, "God is in control." But they fail to acknowledge that we [man] are in authority. Let me explain what I mean. If I say you can borrow my new car and you go out and wreck it, the car is mine, but it was in your possession. That means you are responsible for what happened to it, because I entrusted it to you. The care belongs to me, but the power is in your hand to decide how you will handle it. On my end, I have insurance and extended warranties on my car so that I can fix any damage you may cause. The same goes with the world. God created us from the beginning to walk in dominion. Genesis 1:26 says, "Then God said, 'Let Us make man in Our image, according to Our likeness; let them have dominion over the fish of the sea, over the birds of the air, and over the cattle, over all the earth and over every creeping thing that creeps on the earth." That's why Jesus taught the disciples how to pray. In Matthew 6:10 He said, "Your kingdom come. Your will be done On earth as it is in heaven." What Jesus was trying to show us here was that we [man] are established as partners with God through [salvation in] Christ to welcome God's will in the earth. So, when God is trying to do something or stop something in the earth, He partners with His children through our prayers and through our actions to get it done.

God partners with us [humans] to carry out His work. God's fleshly work was finished on the cross, and He will not do your job for you. God is counting on you to carry out your assignment. God has an expectation of you, not because you can't or because He can't, but because He respects His own Word and the order He set in place.

Faith is the currency of the kingdom of heaven. Mark 11:24 says, "Therefore I say to you whatever things you ask when you pray, believe that you receive them, and you will have them." When you want to receive something from God, you must have faith to get it. Confidence is the tangibility and visibility of your faith. It is time to start looking like what you are believing God for!

I didn't know anyone who was familiar with the territory God had called me to. But I went forward. There may not be a previous example of the path you plan to travel either, because we are all different and unique in the kingdom. God has a plan for each person that will further His kingdom to bring others into fellowship with Him. When God called me to step out on faith, I was so afraid. What the Lord was asking of me required me to become financially independent at a moment's notice—quit my job, step down from pastoring, leave my mother's house, buy a car for the first time, stop working on my bachelor's degree, and start seminary school all within the course of about three months. What was going on in my life was something I had never heard of before. I knew that the next phase of my life would be great, but I shied away from it because of uncertainty. God has given each of us a unique assignment that we are capable of fulfilling because of who He is.

Realize that you may have to set precedent for your next destiny move. You're the bondage breaker. Because the generation before you persevered in prayer, there are some struggles you will not have. Sometimes you have to be okay with blazing your own trail. John 14:4-6 says, "And where I go you know, and the way you know. Thomas said to Him, "Lord, we do not know where You are going, and how can we know the way?" Jesus said to him, I am the way, the truth, and the life. No one comes to the Father except through Me."

Look at that scripture. Jesus is saying to the disciples, 'You know where I'm headed and you know how to get to where I am. Thomas responds, "No we don't!" And Jesus was like, "I am the way, the truth, and the life. The only way to the Father is through me." To me, Jesus is saying—*I AM the journey, I am the foundation, and I am the destination that you want to reach.*

If you know me, you know the way. As I learned to keep my business to myself, people would make comments about how my life lacked direction. They said hurtful things because they couldn't understand the common thread of what God was doing in my life. I had to remind myself often that just because "they" don't know what I'm doing, doesn't mean I don't know what I'm doing. *Their opinions do not mean that God doesn't know what He is doing in my life.* And if you are not careful, you will give people the power to determine who they think you should be. God has a plan. The bible says that the steps of a good man are ordered by the Lord. If you are in a season where you feel like you don't understand what's next, then get to know God on a deeper level. If you know Him, then you know the way. He will show you the journey to His manifested promises in your life.

The Lord may be asking something of you right now that you may have never witnessed before. Sometimes the reason you haven't seen anyone else do what you want to do is because no one else is you. There is an assignment that no one else can do but you. Stop waiting to see someone else do the thing that you are supposed to do first. Even if you haven't seen a precedent for what God wants from you, take my testimony as inspiration to go anyway!

Chapter 6
New Community

Chapter 6: New Community

Psalm 27:10 says, "When my father and my mother forsake me, Then the Lord will take care of me."

When you move out of abusive scenarios, you may feel isolated when you initially decide to step away from the familiar. However, hold on to that scripture (Psalm 27:10) for dear life. When my mom remarried her ex-husband, it felt like someone jammed a dagger through my heart. I began to see myself as flawed because I wondered why *me* being her teammate wasn't enough. I couldn't figure out why she kept choosing him. My image—the way I saw myself, took a hit. I lost inspiration and forgot many of my dreams. I felt like my mom didn't love me enough, and if she gave up loving me, no one else would.

I felt forsaken in the sense of betrayal. I felt so betrayed. I was attacked verbally and spiritually for not agreeing with her decision.

The same concept, but different scenarios, has happened to many others. Your parents may have ignored you to put more focus on the ministry. Those you looked to for love and care may have abandoned you for a drug addiction or not being productive in life. Or maybe you've come from a single-parent home. If that's you, and you have felt rejected, look to the Lord for strength and love just like I did. Remind yourself of His promise in Psalm 27:10. When setting out to blaze a new trail, some of the people you love most will not agree with you in the beginning. Most onlookers will not agree with you until they see you winning. Remember you don't have a point to prove. Just keep following God in the way that He leads you. In the meantime, you will have to learn to make the presence of the Lord your dwelling place. He is who will hide you, secure you, heal you, comfort you, love you, care for you, provide for you, and stay with you. He also sends people who represent His loving intentions for us. The new people God will send to represent Him may be totally unfamiliar to you and unexpected. The best thing you can do is learn to fully accept the new support system that God will send you on your journey. There may not be one person that you can accredit all your help to and that's because the Glory belongs to God.

Romans 8:37 says, "Yet in all these things we are more than conquerors through Him who loved us." Do you see that His love helps us champion all things? That's why basking in the Father's love daily has to become priority, because we cannot operate as "more than conquerors" without knowing that we are loved by God our father.

Romans 8:38-39 says, "For I am persuaded that neither death nor, life, nor angels nor principalities nor powers, nor things present nor things to come, nor height nor depth, nor any other created thing, shall be able to separate us from the love of God which is in Christ Jesus our Lord." Don't ever be convinced that God will love you less because you made a healthy decision for yourself.

I take comfort in the Word. When the Lord led me to that scripture, I just held my bible and cried. Because even in the moment when I felt like a failure, He was still in it with me.

Let me share with you the examples of some of the people that God sent to represent His loving intentions for me along the way. It brings me great joy when I reflect on the people God sent in my life.

1. Dr. T: Dr. T was the first person who told me that God would not be mad at me if I stepped down as pastor, He also told me that God said I never had to return to an abusive atmosphere again. That was crucial for me, because at that time, I was not use to having—let alone acting—on my own opinion.

2. Pastor John: I had just quit my job to attend CFNI. I was temporarily working at Daystar Television. He had learned that I started bible college, and I guess I reminded him that his seminary experience was the best years of his life. He would send me money for textbooks and bought me a comforter for my dorm. He would always check to see if I needed anything financially. He and his church gave over $2,000 towards my tuition and necessities. He would always ask how I was doing and even gave me gas money. It was a blessing because I had literally left my mom's house with just what I needed for school. He never asked for anything in return. He never coerced me to join his church. He just gave. One time, I was so behind on my school bill, the dean actually wrote and signed dismissal papers because I was behind on payments. Pastor John took up a general offering at his church and raised over a thousand dollars. He came to the school and talked to the finance manager with me and let them know that he and his church were supporting me. He told them that they were "for me and loved me" (those special words again). I was able to get "UN-

dismissed," and they had to rip up those papers, because my bill was paid!

3. Mr. Bill: I met Mr. Bill and his daughter when I was nineteen. He paid my first payment to get into CFNI so that I could get my keys. I was staying at this lady's house from my spiritual father's church, in the hood. I was like, "Lord, if Mr. Bill doesn't come through with this money, Lord Jesus!" I'm not too big on asking people for stuff, but I didn't have a choice. And I was counting on Mr. Bill to come through. I went up to the school to register with no money. They gave me the keys, and the next day, Mr. Bill gave me the money—$600 and some change. And periodically, when I didn't have the money to pay my tuition, he would sow towards tuition just because he believed in my calling.

4. Linda: Linda was my roommate in school. She represented a turning point in my life, for the better of course. One time I was having a panic attack, because of the pressure from the school bills. I would get so stressed out when I was behind on school. I loved being there so much, but if I were to get kicked out for nonpayment, I didn't have a plan

B. Every time I would get behind on the school bill, which was almost every month, I dealt with a fear of failure. It wasn't just school for me—I literally had nowhere to go. My new home, CFNI was my faith move and my evacuation plan. Going "home" wasn't an option. One day, I was in the kitchen telling Linda how my meeting with the finance director went. She came and hugged me and said, "Majisty, you have to save." *Insert screeching record noise* I was in tears and she was being so super intense. I screamed back at her, "I can't!" Then, I fell down on the kitchen floor and cried! She said, "Yes you can." She was the first person who didn't "pet" me. She held me accountable. She was the first one who talked with me truthfully about my financial discipline, and she was the first one who didn't make an excuse for me by saying, "Oh you know it's hard out here." She didn't let me make excuses. She held me accountable financially. Her parents are financial advisors, and she asked her mom to talk to me to help me get my finances together. She gave me her support system. And she told me that if I got kicked out of school, I could stay with her family.

5. Em: That's her nickname of course. Em was one of my first Caucasian roommates. She had what I thought looked like red hair, but for Caucasian people, it was more brownish. She was the first person I had ever told, outside of my pastor at the time, about the strife I had experienced. I was always taught, "You don't ever talk about your issues to anybody. It doesn't matter what's going on." God sent a lot of healing for me through Emily, because she was the first person who took me seriously. She never wrote me off as if I deserved the negative things I experienced. She prayed with me, and when I needed a hug in that season of my life, Em was there. She also taught me to hug. She would give me warnings, "I'm going to hug you now," because physical touch was somewhat foreign to me. She just really loved me. I remember one time we got into a huge argument about who was going to take out the trash. And I was yelling at her and she said, "Majisty, you're yelling at me, and it hurts, and I want you to stop!" I thought to

myself, *OMG nobody has ever communicated with me like this.* She taught me how to talk to people and express myself clearly without yelling. I haven't yelled at any one like that since then... okay, maybe once or twice, but still that's a major improvement. In my interactions with Em, I realized that anger is not power and that addressing my issues would help me heal.

6. Ms. Cindy: Ms. Cindy was a member of Pastor John's church. When I left CFNI, she let me stay with her in Weatherford, Texas. She let me live with her rent free. She came to the school and picked up my stuff. She would tell me it was for a season, and I'd look back on that season of my life and laugh. She just reminded me that the Lord is my provider (shelter). God sent someone who I didn't even know to give me shelter. It was a hard season for me, because I felt like I stepped out on faith, but I also failed. But even in my weakness, God still provided.

God truly does send people to us when our parents, friends, or natural support systems fall short. Although your mom, dad, sister, or best friends may abandon you, God will step in and be the family you need—and send you other siblings in Christ who will love you. Even if you don't have confidence in your situation, have confidence in that simple truth, but most importantly, gain confidence in GOD. God will take care of you.

Chapter 7

Loving Yourself

Chapter Seven: Loving Yourself

You love and treat other people the way you would treat yourself. "And the second, like it, is this 'You shall love your neighbor as yourself," There is no other commandment greater than these." - Mark 12:31. If you are negligent to your own needs, you will most likely neglect the needs of others in some way. If you are excessively hard on yourself, you are likely to be critical towards others. Why? Because the format we use to interact with others is many times the approach that is most comfortable to us, because we've used it on ourselves. In order to effectively love your neighbor, you have to know how to love yourself. You have to learn to love yourself right where you are. Stop allowing yourself to say, "I'll love myself when…" *I'll love myself when I lose weight. I'll love myself when I get my teeth fixed. I'll love myself when I graduate from college or when I start making more money.* If Christ loves you unconditionally, meaning HE has removed every stipulation or reason against loving you, then who are you to set a different standard for how and when you love yourself? You are to love yourself and others with the same love that God extends towards you.

Love yourself through Christ's eyes. Love and embrace yourself through every season: the good and the not so great seasons. We are made in the image of God. First, we should love God. Secondly, we should love ourselves.

If you're in bondage to someone else right now, one reason why is because they may have manipulated you emotionally into thinking that no one will ever love you the way they love you. This is especially true if this person(s) knows your secrets. Moving out of abusive situations will require you to attach to the love of God, because His love and presence will become your new security blanket. When I was bound in unhealthy ministry relationships, many times, I did not realize that I was being mistreated. I don't even think these people truly meant to hurt me. For some, I believe they were continuing unhealthy learned behaviors.

Can I tell you a secret? The anointing does not give anyone a "pass" to mistreat people. If you confront someone on multiple occasions when you feel you were mistreated or embarrassed, that may be a sign of an unhealthy environment or relationship. This happens often with ministry leaders and their younger ministers, staff, or armor-bearers. You should never be afraid of your spiritual leader. If you feel afraid, ask the Lord to show you if that fear is coming from you or something ungodly being projected onto you.

In the bible, 1 John 4:18-20 reads, "There is no fear in love; but perfect love casts out fear, because fear involves torment. But he who fears has not been made perfect in love. We love Him because He first loved us." As I began to ask God how I could love Him more, He told me to just meditate on how much He loved me. When you do that, your spirit will naturally reciprocate more love back to God. If fear is a daily struggle for you, ask yourself, "Have I thought about how much God loves me today?"

"Love your neighbor as yourself…" In order to effectively love your neighbor, you have to know how to love yourself. Even through your own shortcomings, failures, successes, love yourself through Christ's eyes. If you love yourself and put yourself only second to God, then you will have more to give to others. You will find yourself less frustrated and agitated with others.

There are many ways that I learned to exercise self-love. If you are the type of person that gives and gives and people around you never give back, it is time for you to focus on loving yourself. If you don't, you will find yourself jealous of the very people you poured into because they are not giving back—and their cup will appear to be full, while yours is empty. You will find yourself having given to people who have absorbed all you have emotionally, financially, spiritually or even physically to the point that you are empty. You cannot pour from an empty cup. The bible says that you will reap what you sow—not *where* you sow. So, if you are constantly giving out and never getting back, it is because the people you are giving to probably don't have the capacity to reciprocate. Sometimes you may just need to sow into yourself! As I learned to really love myself effectively at every level, I became surprised at how much I had left to give to others. I was able to be emotionally available for others because of how I set boundaries for myself. I noticed that I was no longer easily irritable or frustrated, because I was being kind to myself. I learned to take time for myself, time to be still, time to journal and hear from God, time to quiet myself in His presence, and time without social media. One of the ways I learned to love myself was through nutrition and being a good steward over my body. The small changes will make a difference. For instance, you can make sure you eat breakfast before you clock in and work a full day for someone else's company. Take time to exercise even after a long day, or perhaps you need to go to bed earlier so you can be healthy and energized for the next day. I began to buy books to learn about nutrition and proper diet. I started making lifestyle changes. I started going to the gym and deciding that exercise was my "me time," and I made that a priority. I knew that fitness and nutrition could help me enjoy a better quality of life.

Loving myself effectively helped me to identify others that were not. People will abuse you as much as you allow them to. If you learn to draw boundaries, people will adjust to your standards and move around. When you raise the standard of how you treat yourself, it will help you raise the standard for how you allow others to treat you. People who treat others wrong often do that because they are frustrated and angry and unhappy with themselves. So, that means, if you know how to love yourself unconditionally—the same way Christ loves you—it will be easier to spread that same love you have been giving yourself. If you love yourself well, you will be able to love others well too

Learn to set boundaries. Loving yourself also includes what you will not allow others to do. If you don't know where to start, let me give you an idea. Start with setting boundaries for those who constantly disturb your peace. If there is a particular person who always calls you with drama, without fail, you need to draw stricter boundaries. For example, if I know that Tasha always calls me stressed out and ready to complain and her stress stresses me out, then I will stop answering her calls so early in the morning. Tasha will have to wait until noon and at least let me get some breakfast and a cup of tea before she comes to me ready to unload her problems.

Here's another one: if Tommie only calls you after midnight in a low deep voice saying he misses you, and you become tempted to sin, then stop answering his calls at night. The enemy will always try to hit you when you're vulnerable. Give yourself some breathing room. Whether you need time at night to shake off the day, take a hot bath, and simmer down with a cup of tea, or if you need to ease into the day in the stillness of the morning, stop letting people and circumstances interrupt your peace. The book of Ephesians talks about the "shoes of peace" being a part of the full armor of God. Anytime the enemy comes to steal your peace he is trying to dis-armor you. Satan wants to dis-armor you so that he can defeat you. Don't let him win. Protect your peace!

Chapter 8
Whatever it takes!

Chapter 8: Whatever it takes!

I want to take a moment to talk to you about self-image. Many times, people get the idea that because Christ wants us to walk in the spirit that the flesh is worthless. Just because we are not ruled by the flesh does not mean the flesh is useless. People think that the opportunity for a glorified body when we get to heaven is a license to treat the earthly vessel like trash. Hear this loud and clear: the flesh does have value. The flesh is the vehicle for heavenly activity to be carried out in the earth. Let me give you a few scriptural examples:

1. "Do you not know that your bodies are temples of the Holy Spirit, who is in you, whom you have received from God? You are not your own; you were bought at a price. Therefore, honor God with your bodies." -1 Corinthians 6:19-20
   o This means that we as human vessels have a responsibility to glorify God using our physical bodies.
2. "Who Himself bore our sins in His own body on the tree, that we, having died to sins, might live for

righteousness—by whose stripes you were healed."
- 1 Peter 2:24

- o In order for salvation to take place, God needed to express himself in the flesh by being fully God and fully man at the same time.

3. "So God created mankind in his own image, in the image of God he created them; male and female he created them." - Genesis 1:27

- o Salvation restores us to the state of being created in His image.

When the scriptures refer to not walking in the flesh, that means that the sinful desires and ways of the flesh are not supposed to prevail over the ways of the Holy Spirit. We are not to allow ourselves to be more focused on ourselves than we are focused on God. Yes, the word does teach us to walk in the spirit. However, that does not give us a license to have a poor self-image. Our bodies carry our spirits which is what God uses to accomplish His will in the earth realm. To entertain a negative self-image would mean that you permit the tool God uses to carry out His will to be dysfunctional and ineffective. As far as I'm concerned, that school of thought is an insult to God's power, knowledge, and handiwork. If you want to live a sustained lifestyle of confidence and intimacy with Christ, you have to believe in YOURSELF. Once you accept salvation, it is perfectly biblical to believe in yourself through Christ, because He transforms you into all that you should be and helps you see all that you really are!

Many Christians do not struggle with believing in God. They struggle with believing in themselves! That is why people lack confidence and find themselves subject to abusive circumstances. Let me share a scripture with you that I love. Colossians 2:6-8: "As you therefore have received Christ Jesus the Lord, so walk in Him, rooted and built up in Him and established in the faith, as you have been taught, abounding in it with thanksgiving. Beware lest anyone cheat you through philosophy and empty deceit, according to the tradition of men, according to the basic principles of the world, and not according to Christ."

Be established with faith in God, which as I previously mentioned, once manifested outwardly is confidence. Confidence is the essence of faith.

Your dialogue with God and yourself is very important. Decide in this season not to change what you say about God! If you believed Him to be faithful in the beginning don't accuse God of not being faithful in the middle [of your situation]. Start changing your self-conversation daily in a way that brings Him glory. Do the best you can to love, even yourself, with the love of God. Change what you say to yourself. Remember the woman with the issue of blood said to *herSELF* '*If I may but touch' the hem of his garment I shall be made whole.*' Life and death are in the power of YOUR tongue. You can speak life or death over yourself. You can speak life and death over other situations. Choose to speak life.

When you choose to say what God is saying, all of Heaven's resources are backing you up and your surroundings will have to adjust to the Word of God that you spoke. There are scriptures for everything God wants you to have and all that He desires to do with your life. Whatever you're believing God to do in your life, find a scripture to match what you believe in your heart! God has already left all the Word He was going to give through scripture. Now the work is on you to echo His Word in your life.

Start complimenting yourself. When I began building my confidence, I took some oil from my church and began to anoint myself. I would look in the mirror, pray, and read scriptures over myself, because I felt uncovered by those around me. If you wait for people to give you compliments before you tell yourself the compliment you want to hear, you have given other people too much power because your only source of validation is coming from someone else. Tell yourself the things you want to hear.

During my transition, I was going through a lot of warfare in my mind, and I felt like there was no one praying for me, which is something that I wasn't used to. I had always been a part of churches that emphasized "covering." When I stepped away from those unhealthy ministries, I felt alone and as though no one had my back. I would call different friends in hopes that they could encourage me and say the right things. Then one day the Lord showed me, "You already know what you want to hear, so why are you waiting for someone to tell you what you know is true?" So, I began to write letters to myself in my journal. I would write the perfect notes of encouragement for whatever I needed. Whether it was emotional healing or encouragement for school, I began to write the things I needed to hear. The Lord showed me that validation was important, but because of the season I was in, I would need to validate myself. God had to retrain my way of thinking and functioning, because I was used to being built up by others. I had been constantly praised for my strengths and things I did well, but the moment people didn't approve of my actions, they would get silent. I interpreted their silence as a lack of (my) value. I was in environments where people used validation to manipulate me. God had to break that dependency of validation from others in my life. He taught me how to validate myself through Him and how to encourage myself in Him.

If you are in an abusive situation right now or have been for any length of time, it's probably not all bad. There may be some good in it. That small amount of good is what the enemy has you feeding on because it's the only sense of identity you have. Don't allow a small amount of outside validation that people share at their own convenience to keep you in circumstances that are perverse. Know that when you step out of abuse, you may have to validate yourself through Christ. Don't let people use their approval to manipulate you. I don't care who it is!

Outer confidence is important as well. I want you to remember that everything about you— your thoughts, your personality, your dreams, your talents, and even your external shell are all a part of that which will work to the glory of God. There is someone that you can reach that I can't reach, because you have the personality, the background, and the appearance to encourage them or even win their souls to Christ.

When I was younger, I grew up in the North and was never around a lot of black people. In comparison, I thought my nose was too big and that I was ugly. I looked in the mirror and told myself I was beautiful until I believed it. I still practice this on a day-to-day basis. For instance, I know I look nice when I fix my hair nice, so I would get in the mirror and tell myself all the compliments I wanted to hear. So, once I would get myself dolled up, and I'd look in the mirror and say, "Oooh Majisty, you look so cute girl – You better SLAY!" Or my favorite line to tell myself, "You're killin' the game in Jesus' name!" I knew I needed to be validated, so I had to build myself up in that way. I also complimented myself in the mirror every night before bed with no make-up and my bonnet on. I wanted to make sure that I felt confident whether dressed up and made up or dressed down. How many women do you know that have ended up with the wrong guy all because he told her she looked good? This exercise strengthened me. I soon realized that I had more confidence after doing my "Confidence Confessions" in the mirror. As I validated and prayed over myself, I noticed a change in my demeanor. I started to notice myself becoming more diligent and motivated to exercise and take care of myself. The more I would get in that mirror and tell myself that I had it going on, it made a big difference and I started to notice my confidence change. I realized that I needed to be confident before I left the house verses trying to gain confidence from compliments. Confidence comes from knowing who you are, and it was a big part of my journey. I would declare scriptures like Esther 4:14 to remind myself that this is my time and that if I remain silent on what God was telling me, He would choose someone else. Therefore, I couldn't let fear stop me from walking in my assignment and in my purpose. I would read Deuteronomy 28:13, and say I am the head and not the tail; and I used Hebrews 10:35 to remind myself not do anything without confidence! It was almost like I would soak myself in the blood of Jesus just to be able to go out and do what I needed to do.

I asked God to tell me who I was and He did. I wrote all of those words on flash cards and I stood in the mirror, looked at myself, and rehearsed out loud who God said I am. Some of the things God told me I am that I declare daily, if not multiple times a day, include:

- I am excited about my destiny.
- I have a great Godly future.
- I will not fail.
- I will not quit.
- I will persevere.
- I am confident.
- I am fearfully and wonderfully made.
- I am the head and not the tail.
- I am above and not beneath.
- I am a lender and not a borrower.
- I am in the perfect position to live in the manifested promises of God for my life.
- I am favored by God and man.
- New doors of blessing are open to me.
- Today, my eyes will see the goodness of God in the land of the living.
- I will walk in divine health for all my days.

There is something so powerful about agreeing with what God says about you. Don't let a day go by without repeating and agreeing with what God says about you!

Chapter 9
The Confidence Cluster

Chapter Nine: The Confidence Cluster

Once you are healed, it's time to focus. If you are not focused, then it's time to recalibrate. Readjust in a way that helps you hit your mark. No more excuses and no more setbacks. Your experience with the religious spirit was an attack of the enemy to get you off course and to block you from walking in your purpose. Purpose is *identity in action.* God wants to put you—the real you, who He called you to be, in motion. He wants to introduce the refined you to the world!

One area where many believers fall short is the misconception about purpose, assignment, identity, and destiny. I call this important group of traits The Confidence Cluster. The Confidence Cluster provides us with the spiritual confidence to walk forward in purpose, on purpose, and with a clear understanding of who and what Christ called us to be. I gained so much clarity as the Lord began to sort out these areas for me, because I had it all mixed up at first.

Purpose

I believe that everyone has the same purpose. God's purpose for creating man was for us to love and be loved by God and reflect who He is. We were designed for eternal fellowship and intimacy with God. I believe that Jesus dying on the cross was the greatest expression of God's love for us. We live in faith so we can freely receive His love. I believe everyone was created for fellowship with God. If someone gets saved the day before they die and chooses to receive the love of God, they have fulfilled purpose. They have put themselves in a position to freely receive the love of God, but they may not have fulfilled their assignment. Praise and worship is another way that we exercise purpose. This is why idolatry is such a problem, because it perverts purpose by making people worship something else.

Assignment

Everyone has a different assignment. Your assignment is what God wants you to do based on who you are and the resources He has placed inside of you that stem from your identity. There is something that you can do, that no one else can, simply because they are not you. Your background, your testimony, and all the things that you have worked to overcome will allow you to reach a set of people who only want to hear from you—the exact someone who can relate to their experiences. You may be called to minister to youth because of your honesty, transparency, and ability to listen. You may have the perfect connections to help people get out of domestic violence situations. Or you may have a heart to feed the homeless because you know what it's like to be in that position. You have a responsibility to expand the kingdom of heaven on earth by being a steward of your assignment from God. You will know your assignment because it is connected to your passion. Do you love to see young women walking in purity? Do you love to see marriages come together? Do you hate to see people homeless out on the streets? An indicator of assignment is when something frustrates you. Sometimes the thing that frustrates us most about the world is the thing we are called to fix! For instance, if I feel like I'm being controlled, it frustrates me. But this frustration affirms my assignment to destroy religious strongholds. The things that frustrate you are not always attacks from the enemy. Perhaps you are the solution to a problem, and you're anointed to bring deliverance in that area.

Pay attention to what draws a response from you and what captures your attention. Your assignment may just be staring you right in the face!

Identity

There are three components of identity: physical, spiritual, and personality. Identity includes who God created you to be and your physical make up. There is a physical element to who you are. You may be African-American, Hispanic, Caucasian, male, female, short, tall, and so forth. In addition, the following are included in the personality component of your identity: the way that you think, feel, what frustrates you, what makes you laugh, and your personality. Most importantly, your spiritual identity is what God says about you. Spiritually, you may be a prayer warrior, or prophet, or you may have the gift of administration. Your spiritual identity is often indicated by your spiritual gifts. You may also be spiritually gifted to bring peace and joy wherever you go.

Leaders who try to control and manipulate people are often confusing the four elements that make up The Confidence Cluster: Purpose, Assignment, Identity, Destiny (P.A.I.D). Specifically, they did not know the difference between their ministry assignments and their identities. When a ministry leader does not know the difference between the elements of The Confidence Cluster, he or she may easily fall into offense when someone leaves the ministry or church. This leader will take someone's departure as a sign that they have been rejected as a person. I believe this is when conflict arises—when people can't separate their personal identities from their ministries. Families and churches are ruined when there is confusion about this.

The Lord taught me about The Confidence Cluster when I attended CFNI. I had just stepped down from being a pastor and left the church I was attending. By that time, my ministry hit rock bottom, and I hit rock bottom with it, because *I thought I was my ministry*. When I wasn't being booked as per usual, flying here and there, and getting paid the way I was accustomed to, I thought I was a failure. These ministry activities had to be stripped from me in order for me to realize that the Father still loved me, Majisty Dennis, as a person. He loves me for who I am. He loves my goofiness, my jokes, the dreams that I have, the things I aspire to do, and the way that I love people. He intentionally fashioned me in a special way! He still loves *everything* about me, even if my itinerary is not full.

Destiny

Destiny is where we end up based on the choices that we make. Simple as that. Jeremiah 29:11 declares "For I know the plans I have for you, declares the Lord, plans for welfare and not for evil, to give you a future and a hope." Salvation and faith in God provide us the opportunity to dwell in His presence and experience His promises, but He gives us a choice. God does not violate our free will. He is a gentleman and does not force Himself on anyone. So, He provides us with assignment and purpose, but we all have a choice of whether or not we will carry it out. God provides us with talents and an anointing to increase whatever we have (and multiply this increase). Consider Matthew 25:14-30 with the parable of the master who gives his servants the talents. Each servant was given a different amount of talents. No matter how small or large the number of talents, the master was happy as long as they increased what they were given. The one who did nothing with his talent was called wicked and slothful. In the same way, God expects us to return to Him an increase on the assignment He gave us. In other words, whatever God puts on your heart—pursuit it so that you can walk in the fullness of God's intentions for you. Don't leave your harvest on the table. Following God's way leads to increase.

Think of yourself as the steward of the resources God has deposited into you, and the way you steward your gifts has the potential to add great value to your life and others'.

Once I understood The Confidence Cluster, I noticed other people who were secure in themselves as well. My old CFNI roommate, Michelle, is secure in her identity, and she has an amazing confidence about her. She really knows the difference between the four. She is so comfortable with her identity and it's a joy to be around her. By observing her lifestyle, I noticed that even if she didn't do the right thing, the Lord still loved her. But of course, more often, I've watched her do the right thing knowing that the Lord loves who she is. When you learn to segment these four areas of your life, the enemy's attacks of condemnation will not prosper against you.

If you fail at your assignment, that does not mean YOU are a failure. Your destiny is what you make it with God on your side. Your past becomes irrelevant because you can use your now moments to move into a brighter future.

Identity Confessions

As I began to ask God to show me who I was, He answered me! As I mentioned, I wrote down what the Lord spoke to me on flash cards. I would get in the mirror and declare them over myself every morning and every night. I encourage you to do the same. To start you out here are a few confessions to get you started:

I am fearfully and wonderfully made.

I am smart.

I am a joy to be around.

I am loved.

I am creative.

I am sensitive.

I am strong.

I enjoy spending time with God.

God enjoys spending time with me.

I know my gifts and talents.

I am confident.

I am loving.

I am good at conflict resolution.

I am the head and not the tail.

I am above and not beneath.

I am in the best position in my life to live in the promises of God.

I am driven.

I am organized.

I am a blessing to those around me.

In Jesus Name, Amen.

Chapter 10
Myth-Breakers

Chapter Ten: Myth-Breakers

About the time that I was emerging out of my trial in Weatherford, Texas, God began blessing me. As God was blessing me, people started getting jealous. I noticed people who were okay when times were rough and I was struggling seemed to be mad when I purchased a new car. I could tell that because they knew my struggle in certain areas that they wanted every part of my life to reflect 'struggle'. Thankfully, God did not let that happen! That's when I realized there are some people who will support you as long as you are not doing better than them.

People will try to manipulate you into fitting into their idea of humility. Jealousy is usually the underlying cause. You have to resist the temptation to downplay your greatness and your anointing to make other people feel comfortable. I'm not telling you to go around trying to convince other people of your value. More importantly you have to refuse to sluff of the power of your potential for the fear of being perceived as haughty or high-minded.

There is nothing humble about pretending you don't know the magnitude of your purpose, your assignment, or your God-given destiny. Acting like you don't know who you are and what God said about you is not humility. It's stupid and it will cost you! Have you ever thought about this: the enemy can come to us with a lie, just one lie, and we believe it the first time even though everything the enemy says is completely wrong? But when God comes to us with a promise or a word of truth, we act like we need ten confirmations before we believe.

One time I overheard another young lady having a conversation. She was telling someone, "You're not supposed to say good things about yourself. That's so cocky; you're supposed to stay humble." I thought to myself, this girl couldn't believe a bigger lie! You add nothing to your life by pretending not to be aware of your value. There is nothing to gain and everything to lose by acting like we don't know our gifts and abilities.

Expressions of False Humility

False humility is when we pretend that we are unsure of who we are, or what God spoke to and about us, or even unsure of the promises of God over our lives in an attempt to appear humble. Pretending to be unaware of the move of God and the Word of God after He has already spoken is false humility. Anytime we speak against the high aspirations of others or ourselves in order to appear more holy, that is operating in false humility. When people refuse to go after a dream because it seems beyond their reach, and say they are being "practical," they are demonstrating false humility. Refusing to validate yourself or others for the fear of arrogance is false humility. False humility is a seed of ungodliness that enters through the spirit of religion and disguises itself as humility.

False humility also enters through the spirit of fear. The enemy would try to make you afraid to rejoice in good times for fear that bad times are around the corner. We have to reject the "what goes up must come down mentality in our lives." You can overcome that fear by choosing to rejoice boisterously! Psalm 34:2 says, "My soul shall **make its boast** in the Lord; The humble shall hear *of it* and be glad." Use your confidence in God's faithfulness to rejoice; knowing that He will never fail you. I applied this principle and used it as my courage to be blessed when other people looked at me as if I shouldn't believe in God or my greatness because I was struggling. NEVER-EVER stop boasting in the Lord. Decide you will consistently rejoice in Him and be glad through every circumstance. Just because you're going through a bad time doesn't mean God has forgotten you!

Insecure people will always want those with confidence to stoop to their level to make them feel more comfortable. If we are to be good stewards of The Confidence Cluster God has provided us, we have the responsibility to be consistently confident and determined that we will not turn down our "it factor" for anyone. Remind yourself of Hebrews 10:38, "Now the just shall live by faith; But if anyone draws back, My soul has no pleasure in him." That means it displeases God when we draw back from expressions of our faith through confidence. Stay rooted in your identity through Christ no matter where you are.

The enemy wants to plant jealousy in us. If you are ever faced with jealousy, remember to stay in your own lane. You have to run your own race. Comparison is the first stage of jealousy. Comparison is also the enemy of contentment. If the enemy can cause you to become discontent about your circumstances, he knows you'll accept jealousy next. When you see jealousy trying to creep upon you, the best thing to do is to take yourself out of the equation. People become jealous when they want what someone else has. You can avoid jealousy by keeping yourself out of the equation and refusing to compare your journey to anyone else's. To fight these feelings, declare by faith, "I refuse to compare myself to others, in Jesus' name."

Too often, jealousy robs people of their moments. The jealous spirit can rob us of all the goodness coming to us in the present season because it twists our perception. If we are too focused on what God is doing in others' lives, we will miss what He is doing in ours. Jealousy also works as a repellant for the blessings we really want. To pray for blessings because of jealousy is like asking God to bless covetousness. Some people aren't receiving the blessings they want because they aren't asking God to bless them based on their own needs or desires. Jealous people are likely to pray with no fruit because they are not asking God to give them the blessing that belongs to them. They are asking God to give them the blessings that belong to someone else.

Have you examined your heart about why you are asking God for the things you are asking for? Are you asking for blessings because you want to 'one up" the next person? You have to run your own race and your own journey, and the best way to stop being jealous is to stop comparing yourself to others.

Let me give you some examples of how to counteract jealousy with examples from my own life. I can't be jealous of all my friends who are getting married, because the Lord is still working on me and preparing me to be a wife. There are still more things about singleness that I can enjoy. I finished my bachelor's degree at the age of twenty-four. If I compared myself to others, I could become jealous of so many people who graduated at twenty-one. I could have become discouraged to the point of quitting. Instead of going down that route, I focused on what I have overcome. I overcame homelessness and several seasons of attack and just plain drama. I enjoyed the opportunity set before me. I benefited from the college experience that I always wanted. When I view my situation that way, I feel joy and not jealousy.

Know who to share your joy with. If you start to feel like the people around you are jealous, it's time to switch up your circle. That doesn't mean to cut everybody off. You do not have to make an "I'm cutting people off!" announcement. It means that it's a different season and it may be time to hang out with people on a level above you, because if truth be told, the people who hate on you are usually not doing better than you. As you grow in confidence and in your accomplishments, you will need to reevaluate where you stand with the people at that time. When God starts blessing and you discover that jealous people are around you, that's when you need confidence the most! It takes confidence to be blessed.

When it is time to be blessed, most likely, you will have people who are not on the same level as you, so you will have to rise (in character and spirituality the most). You may have people saying, "Oh we went to the same high school, why does she have a new house?" Or, "We come from the same blood line, and you're making all that money and you think you're too good now." When you finally get to the level that God wants you to operate on, consistently, in many ways, you're going to be a different person. There are things about my finances today that I don't even entertain anymore. When I changed the way I managed my finances a few years ago, my credit improved. That's what allowed me to drive the car I have now. There are things that I don't entertain, which in seasons passed, I may have had time for. For example, I don't have time to hear gossip, because I am a student, so I need that time to focus.

When you find that other people are jealous of you, remind yourself of Isaiah 60:1, "Arise, shine; For your light, has come! And the glory of the Lord is risen upon you." When people hate on you, just keep shining!

Over the years, I have met a lot of people who worked hard for others to receive their breakthroughs. They prayed and fasted with their "loved ones." But once it was time to walk in new levels, those same people attacked the very people they prayed with. Be careful not to attack the very answer you prayed for! People attack what they don't understand. I've personally experienced this. People have prayed for me to become successful, and then they turned and attacked me with their words and actions because I walked in success in a different way than they imagined. Although it was very hurtful, I survived and learned a lot through those seasons.

Chapter 11
Celebrating

Chapter Eleven: Celebrating

One of the best things you can do is learn to celebrate others! It will bring more joy in your life and build your relationships in amazing ways. Sometimes people just need to know someone is "for" them and that someone is cheering them on and hoping they do well. Anytime you get ready to do something for others remember to take yourself out of the equation. If not, you will be conflicted with thoughts like, "When is my time?" "I wish someone would do this for me." In that moment of giving and celebrating the next person, you need to be focused on serving them, not entertaining your own selfish desires. It is easier to celebrate people when you take yourself out of the equation.

As you've been reading this book, you probably realize that celebrating others is a part of your expression of confidence. As believers, we should be excited and look for opportunities to celebrate our brothers and sisters who are walking boldly in their purpose or making waves for God! Too often however, I find that people who are bound by the religious spirit feel like they have to tear others down to build themselves up. The New International Version of Hebrews 10:38 reads, "But my righteous one will live by

faith. And I take no pleasure in the one who shrinks back."
A common misconception about Philippians 2:3(Let nothing be done through strife or vainglory; but in lowliness of mind let each esteem other better than themselves.) is that you have to down play yourself to build others up. That's why people don't practice it like they should. To celebrate someone is to focus on their strengths, gifts, and positives. When doing this, we take ourselves of the equation to ensure that we don't fall into that enemy's trap of comparison.

I touched on comparison in the last chapter, but I want to re-iterate some important points that also relate to celebrating others. Comparison makes celebration impossible. If you fall into the trap of comparison, you will do yourself a great disservice. You may be thinking, *I'm good in that area. I don't compare myself to others!* If so, don't be so quick to write this off. Comparison does not just occur in negative ways that have jealous undertones. Comparison can sometimes be disguised as self-confidence. Imagine this. Have you ever told yourself, "No one is smarter than me." Or, "No one is a better entrepreneur (or coach, minister, musician) than me." This may seem like a way to build yourself up, but statements like these can be harmful. These mentalities rob us of the greatness that other people can add to our lives. If you or I constantly think that no one is smarter, more skilled, favored, or talented than we are, we will never grow and benefit from others' gifts—because we will diminish their value. Everyone has some attribute that we can learn from, even our worst enemies!

Comparison is not the only confidence culprit to look out for. Closely related is the thief of competition. Competition is the greatest expression of insecurity, and sadly, when we compare, we compete. As I processed this school of thought in my mind, I decided that I am incomparable. I'm so amazing in my own right that I cannot and should not be compared to others. When you decide to be incomparable it becomes impossible to compare yourself to others. It's like comparing apples to oranges. They're just not the same. Let me show you how I put this principle into practice. My friend Lisa is a makeup artist. She's very good at makeup, and I always thought I did a decent job at doing makeup as well. So instead of saying, "Lisa is better than me at doing makeup," I took myself out of the equation and said, "Lisa is the bomb at doing makeup." One night, we sat down and had a girl's night in, and since I was *so impressed* by Lisa's makeup skills, I asked her to show me some of her best techniques. We spent the next couple of hours having lots of fun. She shared her passion for makeup, and I learned new application methods. Recognizing her strengths gave me the opportunity to become better at doing my own makeup. And all I had to do was give her the credit she deserves! If you see someone who has something you want or is further along in an area, don't let it make you insecure or hesitant to approach that person to learn from them. Instead of comparing yourself to others, allow their strengths to take you higher. There should be no competitors, only collaborators.

Start today by celebrating others. Begin by telling the people in your life the good things you recognize in them. Start telling others they're awesome and why you think they're awesome. Tell them how you value them and what they mean to you. You will notice that it improves your mood and your demeanor even when you're not paying attention to it. It will help you build community and make friends as well. Celebrating others is key to building unity! If someone has an opportunity and new doors are being opened to them, make sure you're with them in the rejoicing moments. When my friends receive good news, I do my silly dance for them. Be dramatic and extra and let them know you're happy for them. It pushes depression, jealousy, and sadness away because you're taking every moment to be happy, even if it's not your moment.

If my new friend Theresa starts a new job, I could suggest that we go to dinner to celebrate—her treat (LOL). I could get her a card, send her some flowers, and be in that moment with her. The enemy would love to make you feel like you don't have enough or as if your efforts don't amount to anything. Satan wants you to think you have no reason to be happy. Celebrating other people reminds us that we have love to give. Celebrating others is a counter-attack. When you choose to rejoice with others, you automatically get to be twice as happy.

If you have ever left networks of people who were bound by a religious spirit, you were probably accused or isolated when you attempted to break free. People you thought were friends and cared for you may have ignored you. During times like these, the attack from the enemy can leave you feeling really lonely, but rejoicing with others will help you climb out of the pit of seclusion and appreciate the reality of the situation—God loves you. He sends a community of people who will love and celebrate you too.

Chapter 12

The Journey Home

Chapter Twelve: The Journey Home

Sometimes we have to validate our own journeys, and realize that our personal stories are enough. We don't have to make the story any more or any less than what it is.

People ridiculed me for living holy and serving God out of their own jealousy. I don't know how church people managed to preach holiness, but when someone actually lived holy in their presence, they spoke against me and told me I wouldn't make it. "Church people" sent me the message that nothing I did would ever be enough. It was a double standard that confused and discouraged me.

I want you to know that your testimony is enough. The situation I was in causes a lot of church girls to buy into the curiosity of sin, because the religious system has convinced them that living right is not enough. Thankfully, that is not how I ended up.

As I've mentioned before, I was so distraught and confused by this at one point that my mom told me, "Majisty, you don't have to go out and get a testimony." She knew what people were saying to me and how much it hurt. Her words are timeless and relevant even today, so I'll share that same wisdom with you: you do not have to go out and give God problems to solve. You don't have to get sick to know that the Lord is a healer, and you don't have to get in trouble to know that He is a deliverer. This is so important. You may have a *deeper* knowing because of experience, but who God is will never change. You don't need any circumstance to make God more God.

I also want to tell you that God wants you to have a good life. People make it seem like you have to have a certain type of struggle to get to a better place in life. People condemn those who don't have traumatic experiences by insinuating that if we don't experience certain things, we aren't black enough, not real enough, or not successful enough. The Lord knows your portion. Work with whatever you've got. You do not have to walk yourself into trouble to have a testimony.

The words of others and how they define us can truly become hindering blocks if we let them. I've learned that people will doubt you and talk bad about you, and just because you are in ministry or "the church" you will not be excluded. What people say can truly affect your mindset and beliefs about yourself. As Joyce Meyer describes, the mind is our battlefield. We must win the battles in our minds in order to display confidence. The negative talk from others can affect our minds, but there are some techniques that will help you overcome those mental giants. One of the best ways to overcome naysayers is to tell yourself what you wish you could tell everyone else. Sometimes we feel like we need to tell other people so they can understand our perspectives. We feel the need to explain. However, I learned that just the opposite is true. Often, when we feel the need to explain our points of view to others, we really need to say those same things to ourselves until we believe. Resist the temptation to become preoccupied with telling someone else what you should be telling yourself.

When I left my small church to begin life at a new church home, with over thirty thousand members, people had a lot of snide things to say. I know I heard from God when He told me to attend this church. But after hearing other people's comments and two cents, I felt so bad about my decision to leave. I had a moment, and I had to confirm myself. I wrote in my journal, "I was right about going to my new church. I was led by the Lord." From this experience, I learned that we have to be careful about arguing other people's opinions in our minds. I sought the Lord's guidance before transferring my membership and then I started to feel suspicious, conflicted, and tormented because of other people's opinions. It wasn't that I needed to argue other people's opinions aloud or defend myself, I needed to *know* and confirm my decision in my own mind.

The Lord has continued to confirm things for me. I was right for enrolling in CFNI. I was right for other decisions that I made. When you hear God, don't second guess yourself. Even if you are wrong, you have to make a decision and stick with it, because you can't have two minds. If you were wrong, be wrong. If you were right, be right. But don't go back and forth. James 1:7-8 warns us, "For let not that man suppose that he will receive anything from the Lord; he is a double-minded man, unstable in all his ways." Know that even if you make the wrong choice, God will direct your path to get back on track!

Chapter 13
Vindication!

Chapter Thirteen: Vindication!

Late one night as I was getting off of work, the Lord told me to pray for vindication. At the moment, I didn't even know what vindication was, but I prayed it anyway! Vindication: to clear as from an accusation, imputation, suspicion. To afford justification. To assert, maintain or defend against opposition.

The next day, I went to class and the teacher presented us with a prophecy that said for those who had suffered hardship in trial over the last seven years because of witchcraft in the church, God was bringing vindication, and the next seven years would be full of vindication, jubilee, and healing. I cried like a baby that day. My friends were with me crying because I had just told them what God had me praying about the night before!

One of the most beautiful moments when God is bringing you from religion to revival is when He vindicates you! Boom—just like Joseph, God brings you out of the dungeon (Genesis 37-50). The moment when vindication begins seems like you are seeing the light again. God confirms to you and to others that He was with you the entire time!

Remember that vindication is going to require integrity on your part. You will have to walk in the integrity as God favors you. Know that like Joseph, the Lord may still have you serving and stewarding the people who treated you wrong. Even after Joseph arose in power and his brothers betrayed him and sold him into slavery, Joseph still took care of their every need, even after their father died.

There's a responsibility to steward the favor that the Lord gives you, even after you've been vindicated. You have to completely let go of your desire for revenge. Remember that in the same way that God can have mercy on you, that same God is going to extend mercy toward those who have opposed you. God never serves a judgement without a warning first. He will always allow people the opportunity to get it right, because His character is just. When God extends that warning to those who have wronged you, you need to prepare yourself for them to heed. It should be your hope for them to reconcile with you. Allow yourself to be patient in the reconciliation process, because (more important than you being right) there's a special opportunity for healing to come in that place. The religious spirit doesn't attack you through secular people. It attacks you through God's children, so you have to leave room for reconciliation, because we only have one enemy and that is Satan.

When reconciliation takes place, you may have to renegotiate the boundaries of the relationships that were affected, because of other people's dysfunction. You cannot allow yourself to be manipulated the way you were before. Allow me to give you an example.

One year on Thanksgiving, my stepfather went to the hospital. He had collapsed and later learned that he had several blood clots in his lungs. The doctor told him that people never come back from that severe illness. "God spared your life for a reason, you better find out why," the physician warned. During that Thanksgiving, I felt like death was near our family. I started fasting, and I was praying against it. I didn't know who it was, but I prayed as if it were happening to me, but it was him going through that hard time. But I thank the Lord that He answers prayers.

Shortly after, my step father's birthday was approaching. Because of his recent challenges with this health, his forty-ninth birthday was a big deal. My mom asked me to attend the birthday party. At first, I didn't feel any prick or urge to attend. In fact, I didn't want to go at all. Later, my mom told me that the birthday party was at the church (where I once pastored) that I had left. And let me assure you that since my departure, it is very rare to find me in my mom's church. What put the icing on the cake and should have secured my "no," was that she had planned this birthday celebration at 11 a.m. on a Sunday. Now, although my flesh had me ready to say no, I simply told my mother that I would be late, so that I didn't have to miss my church service.

Needless to say, I dreaded going to that party. I was shaking in my car, and I wanted to turn my car around so many times. I thought, *I don't have to do all of this. I don't have a point to prove.* But I had a feeling that this situation would have something to do with reconciliation. So I prayed in tongues all the way to the church.

When I arrived, my mom pointed to a lady and instructed me to sit next to her. I did not want to sit next to her, so I went to the front and sat next to my older stepbrother. He whispered to me and told me that I may have to speak on the mic. I was like, "No I ain't!"

The other ministers were praying over my stepdad. He fell out. My mom stood up to close the service, and sure enough she asked me to say the closing prayer. I paused and hesitated for a moment, but felt like I should go ahead and do it, so I went to the pulpit, and I said the prayer. I prayed a blessing over the church. I prayed that long life and strength of days would be my stepdad's portion.

As I was returning to my seat, after closing out the service, he grabbed me by the hand, and tears were streaming from his eyes. He said, "Majisty, I just want to say that I am sorry if I offended you. If I ever did anything to hurt you, I am sorry. If you believe what I said to you to be a curse [He had told me that no man was ever going to want me], I uproot it in Jesus' name. You are a beautiful person… and he's [my future husband] coming." He continued to explain that he had no examples and no one leading him and teaching him "how to have a Godly family."

I accepted his apology, and I forgave him and thanked him for what he had said. I knew that the Holy Spirit had moved him to say those words to me. The incident that he apologized for had happened almost ten years prior. He had asked me to wash dishes, and I didn't want to. He then told me that, no man would ever want me. His words hurt me to my core. After that, I always wondered if those words were still hindering me like a curse.

Even during the period when he divorced and remarried my mom, he said that I was out of order for disagreeing with that. He told me my spirit wasn't aligned and that God put him in my life. At the time when they remarried, I was still hurt and he had never apologized to me (or my siblings) for all that he put us through when he divorced my mom, put us out, and pushed us into homelessness. If you can put this all into perspective, you can imagine why his apology and our reconciliation that Sunday morning was a big deal.

When you depart from a church or consider departing, and the people within the ministry curse you, realize that the congregation is dealing with witchcraft. Those are not actions that align with the Holy Spirit. The Word of God never tells us to go back and get revenge. As a matter of fact, the bible says in Psalm 139:8, "If I go up to the heavens, you are there; if I make my bed in the depths, you are there." That lets me know that the Lord is with me wherever I go. He will never leave me nor forsake me, but He does not instruct me to seek revenge.

It is possible to disagree and still bless people. I know it was the Lord who put that prayer in me to bless even someone I considered my enemy. If you've been rejected, cast out, or mistreated; the first thing you should do is forgive. Forgiveness is the first decision that begins the healing process. God can handle the rest from there.

Along with vindication comes the opportunity for reconciliation. Remember that forgiveness takes one, but reconciliation takes two. Be open to making things right. We only have one enemy and that's Satan. No matter how bad you were hurt or how much the religious spirit attempted to destroy you, once God presents an opportunity for you to reconcile with another (or other believers), you must do so. Always remember that your battle is not against each other. As the Apostle Paul teaches in Ephesians 6, we do not wrestle against flesh and blood. We fight against spirits, principalities, and sometimes, spiritual hosts of wickedness in heavenly places. Remember, people are not your enemy-the demonic spirits that bind them is what opposes you. Decide not to hold a grudge against them so that God can work in that relationship according to His will.

Your experience may be like what happened to Joseph and his brothers, but you may have to carry yourself like David did when Saul set out to kill him in 1 Samuel 18-24. Saul was considered a leader to David, yet he wanted to kill him. David spent years running from Saul's wrath. When the opportunity presented itself for David to kill Saul, he still didn't take it (1 Samuel 24). He let Saul know that he spared his life. When David did not go in for revenge, it marked the moment that Saul acknowledged that David was more righteous than he and would be the next king. We all know where that lineage led to (eventually Jesus). Regardless of if you are right or wrong, refuse to resort to spite and revenge. God can fix and reconcile situations better with His hand than you ever could by yours.

***

Can I tell you that the prophecy about vindication came to pass? Vindication has been taking place in my family, in my ministry, and in my education and career. As I forgave the people who wronged me, I can honestly say that nothing I desired to do has been hindered. I completed my bachelor's degree. I drive the car I want and live in the home I dreamed of having when I was homeless. I have a great career. My ministry is thriving and I am pursuing my dreams. My soul makes its boast in the Lord! My testimony is that everyone in my family is wholeheartedly trying to do better-even me. Step-by-step, we are forgiving, reconciling, and communicating. We each work harder to build each other up in love. My mom and I now have the strength to confront our issues little-by-little, and we are able to hear one another. My step dad extended the opportunity for me to have nearly $50,000 over a period of time. He became one of my most consistent financial supporters when I attended Dallas Baptist University to complete my bachelor's. My family respects me in new ways, and things will only get better. If you're reading this book, I'd say my ministry is still blessing people and touching lives. God is faithful to his promises! The same way God has been faithful to me, He will be faithful to you!

I want you to remember that God's Word tells us we can win with confidence. Confidence in God, His plan, and who He made you to be will sustain you in rocky places! Let confidence be a bridge for you in every season. You know that you are hearing from God! Confidence will open new doors for you. It will bring you into new healthy relationships. It will help you maintain a standard in all that you do. Confidence will develop the relationships you already have into something that is more beautiful.

Confidence postures you to make God smile. Most importantly, confidence is sustained through a place of intimacy with God. Be confident enough to stand in all that God has spoken over your life.

Confidence Concordance

Use this concordance to remember what the Word of God has to say about Confidence.

- Hebrews 10:35-39: Therefore do not throw away your confidence, which has great reward. For you have need of endurance, so that when you have done the will of God, you may receive what was promised. For yet in a very little while, He who is coming will come, and will not delay. But my righteous one shall live by faith; and if he shrinks back, my should has no pleasure in him. But we are not of those who shrink back to destruction, but of those who have faith to the preserving of the soul.

- Isaiah 30:15: This is what the Sovereign LORD, the Holy One of Israel, says: "Only in returning to me and resting in me will you be saved. In quietness and confidence is your strength. But you would have none of it.

- Hebrews 4:16: Let us then with confidence draw near to the throne of grace, that we may receive mercy and find grace to help in time of need.

- Galatians 5:10: I am confident in the Lord that you will take no other view. The one who is throwing you into confusion, whoever that may be will have to pay the penalty.

- Philippians 1:6: Being confident of this, that he who began a good work in you will carry it on to completion until the day of Christ Jesus.

- Proverbs 3:26: For the Lord will be your confidence And will keep your foot from being caught.

- 1 John 5:14: This is the confidence we have in approaching God, that if we ask anything according to his will, he hears us.

- Isaiah 32:17: The fruit of that righteousness will be peace; its effect will be quietness and confidence forever.

About the Author

Serving in various capacities as God's millennial voice to the world; Majisty Dennis is what the world has been waiting for. Majisty's endeavors range from creative entrepreneurship through her mime ministry to motivational speaking and preaching just to name a few. Having studied at Christ for the Nations Institute and graduated from Dallas Baptist University; she refuses to be defined by societal norms; Majisty is "the edge" where ministry meets the marketplace. Her creative talents have led her to touch hundreds of thousands of lives through national television, radio, live presentations, and concert productions. She travels the country inspiring others to carry out their assignment without excuse and shares strategies on how to do so! Majisty communicates passionately through speaking, mime, and her life changing literary works. Above all, Majisty is a voice echoing the heart of God. With a focus on confidence and intimacy with Christ; Majisty poured her heart into her newest book "From Religion to Revival." The book is designed to help others delve into the heart of God and live a life that reflects His presence. With a gift from God packaged in a way the world has never seen before-this millennial is on a mission. Majisty will never stop inspiring revival in the hearts of many.